THE BATTLE
—— FOR ——
SOULS

STEVEN TREADWELL

Copyright © 2023 Steven Treadwell.

All rights reserved. No part of this book may be reproduced, stored, or transmitted by any means—whether auditory, graphic, mechanical, or electronic—without written permission of both publisher and author, except in the case of brief excerpts used in critical articles and reviews. Unauthorized reproduction of any part of this work is illegal and is punishable by law.

ISBN: 979-8-88640-454-8 (sc)
ISBN: 979-8-88640-455-5 (hc)
ISBN: 979-8-88640-456-2 (e)

Because of the dynamic nature of the Internet, any web addresses or links contained in this book may have changed since publication and may no longer be valid. The views expressed in this work are solely those of the author and do not necessarily reflect the views of the publisher, and the publisher hereby disclaims any responsibility for them.

One Galleria Blvd., Suite 1900, Metairie, LA 70001
1-888-421-2397

CONTENTS

Introduction v
Chapter 1   God set Boundaries We Cannot Pass 1
Chapter 2   Don't Live in Willful Ignorance 9
Chapter 3   Environmental Integrity 15
Chapter 4   Keep Your Focus on God 18
Chapter 5   Live a Repentant Lifestyle 27
Chapter 6   Understanding Jesus as God 30
Chapter 7   Jesus is the Name of God 45
Chapter 8   Idolatry 53
Chapter 9   We all Have Boundaries 61
Chapter 10 Do You Know Who You Are? 74
Chapter 11 Learn these Scriptures for Growth, Prosperity, and Success in Life! 80
Chapter 12 Develop a Personal Relationship with God 81
Chapter 13 You Can Change Things by What You Say 83
Chapter 14 How to Move Mountains Out of Your Life 85
Chapter 15 Holiness was Here Before the World Began 95
Chapter 16 Scriptures: of The Mystery of Jesus Christ as God and Father 98
Chapter 17 Cowards 100
About the Author 107

INTRODUCTION

What in Hell is wrong with you? America, there is not a man, woman or group that I want to go to hell with. What about you? Do you have a going to hell partner that you will go to hell and high water with. No, you are not that cool that I want to go to hell with you. Hell fire burning constantly, always, never ending. My question to you is, Are you free from "Mental Kidnapping" the skillful and seductive art of demonic enslavement. The world needs to come out of the prison of their mind and receive "God's Mental Therapy." Keep exercising and practicing the Word of God until you get "God's Mindset." There is a spiritual battle going on inside you for the control of your soul. The battle will determine if you end up in heaven or hell. We don't have as much time as we think because souls are being snatch from this earth all day long. We must be sure about our eternal destiny. We are from eternity and we will return to eternity. So, you choose this day whom you will serve. We have one dance and one chance. We have this one life to live here on earth and after that there will be judgement. You are going to meet Jesus Christ and you are going to meet him as Savior or you are going to meet as judge. One thing for certain and two things for sure, and that is you are going to meet him.

CHAPTER 1

GOD SET BOUNDARIES WE CANNOT PASS

God has a fence around us that we cannot pass because he wants us to do his thoughts. It is the burden of the word of the Lord for Israel. Prophecy is a Divine Prediction for our comfort and benefit. He is the same God who stretched forth the heavens, and laid the foundations of the earth and formed the spirit of man in him.

The evil that you do will be the same evil that will boomerang right back at you. Jeremiah 5:22 says, "Fear ye not me? saith the Lord: will ye not tremble at my presence, which have placed the sand for the bounds of the sea by a perpetual decree, that it cannot pass it: and though the waves thereof toss themselves, yet can they not prevail; though they roar, yet can they not pass over it?"

The scientists who are transforming gender norms by exploring God's creation by making counterfeit men and women are wicked. They practice shaping people's sexual and reproductive health outcomes to give Satan broader opportunities against the standards of God's thoughts. Jehovah has set a boundary that they cannot pass over.

Psalms 148;5-6 tells us to "Let them praise the name of the Lord: for he commanded, and they were created. (Vs.6), He hath also established them forever and ever; he hath made a decree which shall not pass." When man and woman go to their long home and mourners go about the streets, "Then shall the dust return to the earth as it was; and the spirit shall return unto God who gave it" Ecclesiastes 12:7.

We should ask God to teach us to number our days as we pass through life on our journey here on earth. No man knows the day or the hour of his departure and death will be the last stop for all the living. Your spirit, the real you will live an everlasting life in heaven or hell.

There is a group that calls itself GYSI. This group work hard to undue the manifold works that was made and created by the wisdom of God. The Gender, Youth and Social Inclusion frame work are seeking assistance for same sex couples with children and men who want sex changes and drugs that alters men's chest into breast and male sex organs into organs of a woman. GYSI is created to help support the definition of a lie. The meaning of a lie is the way things are situated and arranged to give a false impression. Their purpose is to first deceive themselves and then someone else.

It is a lie because homosexuals cannot reproduce and have children. They are working by experimenting on a way to make a man pregnant in China. The only way a man can get pregnant is by the spirit of God that is placed in him when saved. They want the rights that women have who are murdering their children by abortion. The women are jealous and envying the male authority that God gave to the male.

This is another example of the counterfeit trying to be real. They want medical help. Planned Parenthood clinics are now serving abortion pills where women can keep committing fornication and adultery by having sex as they carry their dead child. Wow! Now they can act out their lust by fornicating and committing adultery by having sex with their dead child in them.

This is an effort to help our government and the medical field working in counseling to help those who are confused. This is where the professional saying comes from that says, "The patient went to see his Psychiatrist, but he was not there because he was gone to see his Psychiatrist." Satan is the author of confusion.

Doctors are being pushed by GYSI to get an understanding of their confusion. This is another extreme effort to make their wrong thoughts equal to God's original plan for man and woman. They are now including children and men in a gender equal world where all people achieve their sexual and reproductive health needs. Misery loves company.

Hell is enlarging itself because misery loves company. How can humankind be so hardheaded when God sent us a scape goat to come out of our sins giving us a way out of our sin? Jesus wants us to be one with him. Balaam told Balak in Numbers 22:18 that "I cannot go beyond the commandments of the Lord, to do either good or bad of my own mind; but what the Lord saith, that will I speak?

Jesus was tempted three times by the devil in the wilderness when he replied, "It is written" three times to the devils 3 temptation or request. We must do Proverbs 3:5-6, "Trust in the Lord with all thine heart, and lean not to unto thine own understanding." (Vs.6), in all thy ways acknowledge him, and he shall direct thy paths."

The spirit that God put into the man Jesus Christ who was born of a woman was the same spirit or the presence of God hovering over the water before the world began in Genesis 1:2. "And the spirit of God moved upon the face of the waters." We have been given the glorious unity of becoming one in the spirit with Jesus Christ who is the Father where all of us are perfected into one. God is spirit and those who worship him must worship him in spirit and in truth. "Acts 4:12 LB tells us that, "There is salvation in no one else! "Under all heaven there is no other name for men to call upon to save them." Jesus Christ name is from everlasting to everlasting.

Stay close to the Lord whatever the cost. It was first in Antioch that believers were called Christians but Christianity came because of confused Roman Catholics that could not, and did not explain the Godhead right and we ended up with 3 gods instead of one. This is where man took it upon himself to call himself a Christian or to be Christ like.

Christ is the anointing and Jesus who is the name of God and the anointed one was here before the worlds began. He made a body in Mary and then got in that body. John 17:24 told God, "Father, I want those you have given me to be with me where I am, and to see my glory, the glory you have given me because you loved me before the creation of the world" NIV.

We all have choices to make but why should your life end in darkness? Our destiny depends on the choices we make and there is no reason to argue with God and blame him. People love celebrations but it is better to celebrate ones death in sorrow that will refine and filter our thoughts about where we are going to end up. We can't stop what we don't know is going to happen. Some people take chances in life without God and choose their own crazy path in life and end up defeated.

They have no hope because all they see is death at the end. Hope is always for the living but those who die or commit suicide become hopeless. When they go to hell there will be no hope. God commanded us when he said "Thou shalt not kill" and that even means suicide or killing yourself. It is written over the portals of hell abandon all hope ye who enter in. Hope is that earnest, intense, favorable, confident expectation. Death is one thing we all have in common. We have that blessed hope when we get saved. We have the hope of eternal life with Christ Jesus.

Those that forget God and turn against their creator will burn in hell. They forget why they are breathing and they forget whose spirit is in their nostrils. Job 27:3, "All the while my breath is in me, and the spirit of God is in my nostrils." Those that tell God depart from us: and what can the Almighty do for us? They think that they were born to be bad having no sorrow for their sins. They don't even be ashamed of their sin.

God will break them of their evil. The land suffers for the sins of its people. The land is defiled by crime because the people have twisted the laws of God. Mathew 11:12 and Hebrew 4:12 Author Paraphrase, God's kingdom has suffered violence and the violent takes it by force. We take it by agreeing with the word of God in Hebrew 4:12 paraphrase that is quick (living) and powerful and sharper than any two edged sword. His word is piercing even to the dividing asunder of soul and spirit, and of the joints and marrow that makes all things but naked and open in His sight. All things are naked and open unto the eyes of God.

When mankind openly rebel then the curse of God comes upon them and the land. When man-kind see the error of his ways he can repent of that sin and return into God's favor. If you return unto the Almighty then in Job 22:28 says, "Thou shalt also decree a thing, and it shall be established unto thee: and the light shall shine upon thy ways,"

In these last days the blood of men will be crying out to God. Isaiah 24:10 tells us how "The city of confusion is broken down: every house is shut up, "The cities lie in chaos and every home and shop is locked up tight to keep out looters." There will be mobs in the streets and gladness has disappeared. After this the city will be left in ruins with evil and treacherous. Mathew 24:10-11, "And then shall many be offended, and shall betray one another, and shall hate one another, (Vs.11), "And many false prophets shall rise and shall deceive many."

When Covid 19 came on the scene all houses was shut up and the streets were cleared. Many had a chance to sanctify themselves and find truth. God honors a clean vessel with prayer and praise. Genesis 8:21-22, "And the Lord smelled a sweet savour; and the Lord said in his heart, I will not again curse the ground any more for man's sake; for the imagination of man's heart is evil from his youth; neither will I again smite any more everything living, as I have done.' (Vs.22), "While the earth remaineth, seedtime and harvest, and cold and heat, and summer and winter, and day and night shall not cease."

The only thing evil men understand is punishment. They believe they will never get caught serving the devil that makes them fall into traps that deceive and fool themselves. They only outwit themselves. God does strange and unusual things to punish his people. They learn by rote, the things of God by repetition but do not obey him. They actually believe that they can hide their plans from God. They think that he don't see them and they can keep him in the dark but God dwells in thick darkness to bring you out of it. They think God who created them is dumb or don't exist because of His grace and mercy. Their cup of sin is almost full.

The fool has said in his heart there is no God. God says in Isaiah 43:13, "From eternity to eternity I am God. No one can oppose what I do." Today, humankind has more knowledge and wisdom than long ago and has determined to himself that he is Jehovah; his own god. This is why calamity and disaster comes suddenly not knowing where it came from. Then they die trapped in their sin with no atonement for their sin. All the demons in hell that they worshiped will not be able to help them then.

Instead of being a terror they will meet the King of Terrors in hell. God brings terror with his judgement. No one knows terror more than the person who died in terror. Psalms 91:8 says, "Only with thine eyes shalt thou behold and see the reward of the wicked." You believed the advisors who study astrology and those who study the stars to save you when they can't even save themselves.

God don't want anybody or anything receiving his glory. God is a jealous God for real. You should give the things that Jehovah has made to be to his glory! Humankind has a sin infection and need God's spiritual hospital to give emergency care to their spirit, soul and body. Job 2:13 tells us "But he is in one mind, and who can turn him? And what his soul desireth, even that he doeth."

People without God that practice sin who are called sinners need to hurry before they self-destruct. They have no talent to do right, but only to do wrong. When you were in distress God heard your cry while you were walking around doing your own thing and you gave him no praise. Don't be ungrateful but give him the glory honor and praise for bringing you out of hurt, harm and danger. "They are those that rebel against the light; they know not the ways thereof, nor abide in the paths thereof." Job 24:13.

God wants us to grow in his grace and wisdom so we can have the victory in our every- day life over every spirit that comes against us, our family, leaders and nation. When you fight against God you will eat the bitter fruits of wanting to have your own way. Life and death are in the power of the tongue and we must watch what we say. We reap the terrors of life when we choose our own way instead of obeying God's instructions.

Children of God must stomp the devil and keep him under their feet no matter who or what he uses to come against their soul. It is not that person but evil spirits using a person or thing as an agent of the devil. God's wisdom is a treasure of knowledge called good sense from a good God. When we walk the pathway of life we will be protected on every side because you will know right from wrong when you are guided by his Word. Be determined to be wise and run from foolishness.

When you develop common sense and good judgement discerning good and evil in the hearts of men wisdom can give you a better life. Wisdom is our greatest teacher because wisdom was here before God formed the earth. Wise men hate evil. Those who refuse wisdom love death. God's wisdom brings success in life. Dis- obedience to Gods wisdom or his word brings the curse where every -thing you do will fail. When we don't follow the wisdom of God we lie to ourselves first.

You are not wiser than the one who made you. People feel comfortable in their sin when they find someone who agrees with their wrong choice. "There is a way that seem right unto man, but the end thereof are the ways of death" Proverbs 14:12. In the beginning God breathed the breath of eternity into Adam. God knows the end from the beginning. Jehovah knows the thoughts and intents of the heart. There are a lot of lazy people who want to keep up with the Jones and will not work but instead covet that of another.

They are in concert with Satan who covets that of another when they rob, steal and kill. Satan wanted what God had. They were deceived by Satan and end up dead or in prison. A wise man once said that a wise youth can come out of prison and succeed and even become king even though he was born in poverty. People love to help people who have made a mistake. We all make mistakes. Our society wants every individual to live up to his or her highest potential and become a success story.

There are movie stars and great lawyers who are great examples. After prison stories include people who were ex-offenders who became success stories becoming attorneys. A lot of men and women go to jail and come out with guilt, shame, and condemnation. In other words they have a victim mentality. They reject the thought of success to the highest point of their potential living with a victim mentality.

Remember Joseph went to prison and went from the prison to the palace. When money becomes your god you never get enough and it begins to take away your sleep. Slaves to money don't sleep very well. Don't waist the spirit of grace that God gives you thru the death of his firstborn from the dead. "Have we not all one father? Hath not one God created us" Malachi 2:10?

CHAPTER 2

DON'T LIVE IN WILLFUL IGNORANCE

The knowledge of God is moving fast around the world. How can a man or woman not know about Jesus Christ the one who cast out demons, raised the dead, make the blind see and the lame to walk. Then the seventy return to Jesus with a praise report in Luke 10:19 telling him how demons were subject to them. Jesus informed them in Vs. 20 to rejoice in something more important and that is, "because your names are written in heaven."

Those who are still practicing sin and know better need to "Repent" admit it, quit it, and get back with it. Get back in line with the word of God. You get in line everywhere else like the bank and grocery store. Why is it so hard for you to get in line with the uncompromising, unadulterated, unchanging word of the Living God.

God manifest his word through preaching. Jeremiah 2:13,"For my people have committed two evils, they have forsaken me the fountain of living water, and hewed them out cisterns, broken cisterns, that hold no water." They have left God and have become spiritually retarded. They have a crack in their cisterns and can't hold water.

In Jeremiah 9:23-24 God says, "Thus saith the Lord, Let not the wise man glory in his wisdom, neither let the mighty man glory in his might, let not the rich man glory in his riches: (Vs.24), "But let him that glorieth glory in this, that he understandeth and knoweth me, that I am the Lord which exercise loving kindness, judgement, and righteousness, in the earth: for in these things I delight, saith the Lord."

We should remember our names are written in heaven with our relationship with God knowing and trusting him. We do this by staying in his presence and this will be our confidence against doubt and unbelief. In our world money is power and it can put you in control of many situations. The love of money in a family church makes the church a family affair especially when family members hold all key positions. How quick we forget what God has done for us. Again and again God delivers us in our sin slavery but most continue until self-destruction.

Is covetousness warring against your mind? Do you want everything that somebody else has without putting in the work? Are you crucified with Christ Jesus? Are your hands nail to the cross keeping you from taking that of another? Are your feet nailed to the cross keeping you from running into mischief?

Do you have the mind of Christ and hold the thoughts feelings and purposes of his heart or are you people pleasing? When you say everybody is doing evil and they are prospering and I am doing what is right and have less than they do. Remember that God hate evil and he will give them grace to come to him before he brings judgement on them.

Joel 2:12 says "Therefore also now, saith the Lord, turn ye even to me with all your heart and with fasting, and with weeping, and with mourning: (Vs.13), "And rend your heart, and not your garments, and turn unto the Lord your God: for he is gracious and merciful, slow to anger, and to great kindness, and repenteth him of the evil." "For I am the Lord, I change not; therefore ye sons of Jacob are not consumed. God is giving all liars and tricksters his grace another opportunity to get it right.

Men turn their heart against God and let cursing come out of their mouth. Men and women of God are being transformed by the renewing of their mind. They are not there yet so God said in Job 15:15-16, "Behold, he putteth no trust in his saints; yea the heavens are not clean in his sight." Remember that God made the heavens and the earth. Lucifer was in heaven and turned a 3rd part of heaven against God. Jehovah had to clean heaven out. In Job 15:16 says, "How much more abominable and filthy is man, which drinketh iniquity like water." We must yield our bodies to be servants of righteousness unto holiness.

Romans 6:16 says, "Know ye not, that to whom ye yield yourselves servants to obey, his servants ye are to whom ye obey; whether of sin unto death, or obedience unto righteousness." Obedience will bring the fruit of holiness and you will end up with everlasting life. God uses your enemies to spank you but sometimes he allows your enemies to have pity on you.

Sometimes you hear evil people who have never bless the Lord say, thank you Jesus. They knew what the penalty of their crimes deserved. They are the ones living in darkness and walking in the shadows of death breathing danger at every turn. We are all one step away from death. Those who rebel against God have no hope. When people die without Jesus Christ they will receive eternal damnation. All they have to do right now is repent and turn from their sin and be baptized in the name of Jesus Christ. Receive the gift of the Holy Spirit, and give Jehovah praise instead of Satan.

Getting money and the praise of men and women makes them forget that there is a hell below. The Toy industry has now become inventors of evil things by making homosexual dolls that Romans 1:30-32 speaks of. "Backbiters, haters of God, despiteful, proud, boasters, inventers of evil things, disobedient to parents, (31), "Without understanding, covenant-breakers, without natural affection, implacable, unmerciful: (32), Who knowing the judgement of God, that they which commit such things are worthy of death, not only do the same, but have pleasure in them that do them."

We should set our mind toward pleasing God so that the love of God is shed abroad in our heart by the Holy Spirit and his love will abide in us richly. We should keep ourselves in the kingdom of light, in love, and in the Word and the wicked one touches us not.

God gets your public praise when you witness about his goodness. Psalms 35:18 says, "I will give thee thanks in the great congregation: I will praise thee among much people." God delights in your testimony when you tell others about his goodness and how he brought you out of your troubles. Bragging on God shows your delight in Him. God loves to be praised as you brag on him by giving your testimony. Talking about Jehovah keeps our conversation in heaven.

When you brag on God you help strengthen your brothers and silence the enemy. Sometimes you can be praying for your enemy and their heart is set on destroying you. They return evil for good and hatred for love. Souls of men and women are only a number to Satan as he uses them up and throw them away. Some die in their sin while others go to jail and die in that way. The enemy only says, Next! The only thing Satan brings to the table is theft, destruction and death and these are called the curse. Satan brings skin and bones and disgrace while you fail at everything you do.

So be strong in the Lord and in the power of his might. Beware of those who will distort the truth to draw a following. God's anger is not like human anger. God's wrath is provoked. Romans 1:18, 22, 25, 31, LB says, "But God shows his anger from heaven against all sinful, evil men who push away the truth from them. "For the truth about God is known to them instinctively; God has put this knowledge in their hearts".

Continue: Vs.22, "Claiming themselves to be wise without God, they became utter fools instead." Vs.25, "Instead of believing what they knew was the truth about God they deliberately chose to believe a lie". Vs.31, "They tried to misunderstand, broke their promises, and were heartless --without pity." Is it not strange that people will take what J Z says and will not take what J C (Jesus Christ) said. J Z is only a puff of smoke and he is only here for a moment and he will disappear. Mankind is only like grass that is cut down and withers away. God gave you and J Z fresh air to breath. This is why all honor and glory belongs to Jehovah.

Romans 2:1,3, & Vs.8,12 LB tells us, "Well you may be saying, what terrible people you have been talking about. But wait a minute! You are just as bad. When you say they are wicked and should be punished, you are talking about yourselves, for you do the same things." (Vs.3), "Do you think that God will judge and condemn others for doing them and overlook you when you do them too?"

(Vs.8) in Romans the 2nd chapter says, "But he will terribly punish those who fight against the truth of God and walk in evil ways — God's anger will be poured out upon them". (Vs.12) in Romans 2 tells us that, "He will punish sin wherever it is found. They know what is right but don't do it. The day will come when the commander in chief Jesus Christ will judge the secret lives of everyone, their inmost thoughts and motives."

Paul said in Romans 2; 24, "This is all part of God's great plan which I proclaim." The world is watching the church and "No wander the Scriptures say that the world speaks evil of God because of you." God is looking for those whose heart is right with him. He is looking for those who have a changed heart and mind from sin to righteousness.

We should all humble ourselves and stand hushed and guilty before the Almighty God. Now we must trust Jesus Christ to take away our sins. This is how we get the not guilty verdict from God. Repentance, Baptism, Obedience and Christ blood along with our faith is the means used to take God's wrath away from us.

Yes, God is even letting criminals go free when they confess their sins and be baptized in the mighty name of Jesus Christ and receive His Spirit. You don't even have to be all good like that because it is not based on how good you are. It is based on repentance, obedience and what Christ has done for us at the cross and our faith.

God treats everybody the same. We are saved by grace through faith and we must trust Jesus and fully obey him. We must keep our imaginations and thoughts of our hearts prepared unto God. Jehovah loves it when it is in thine heart to bless him. He loves it when you represent the Father and Jesus well.

Remember that God's man in the center of God's will is immortal until God is through using him. "And I give unto you eternal life; and they shall never perish, neither shall any man pluck them out of my hand. My Father, which gave them me, is greater than all; and no man is able to pluck them out of my Father's hand (John 10:28,29KJV). The best way to know you're in the hand of God is to do the work that He placed before you to do.

The reward of the wicked and their existence will perish with them from the earth and they will be chased out of the earth. All they ever did was quarrel with God instead of delighting themselves in the Lord. Evil people only have the spirit of lust and that shameful sin is a crime against God that roots out all the good they have planted.

(Psalms 125:3,5) "For the rod of the wicked shall not rest upon the lot of the righteous; lest the righteous put forth their hands unto iniquity." (Vs.5), "As for such as turn aside unto their crooked ways, the Lord shall lead them forth with the workers of iniquity: but peace shall be upon Israel."

Heavenly Father, please lead and guide us into the way of everlasting. It is Jehovah who made you and has given us life and breath. If God were to withdraw his spirit all life would disappear as we know it and mankind would turn to dust. Dust thou art and to dust thou shall return. We know that as soon as our breath leaves our body we are on our way back to dust. God gave you life by giving you His spirit. Don't be ungrateful but show God daily how much you appreciate Him.

God can prevent a vile man from ruling to save a nation from ruin. He can also wipe out an entire nation just as easily. What is so sad is some people still won't repent of their sins which are many. They are even too proud to ask God's forgiveness of their sins when surrounded by plagues like Marburg Virus in West Africa. These viruses are of man. Misery loves company. They have bitterness toward the only one who can save them. We must warn all sinners because God wish that all should be saved and come to repentance.

Meditate day and night on his word so you can become closer to God. Pray to Him. Discover your selves. In 11 Chronicles 7:14 tells us that, "If my people, which are called by my name, shall humble themselves, and pray, and seek my face, and turn from their wicked ways; then will I hear from heaven, and will forgive their sin, and will heal their land." These four steps to humble, pray, seek his face, turn from sin are key steps to answered prayer and getting God's goodness.

CHAPTER 3

ENVIRONMENTAL INTEGRITY

We need to listen while it is still time. God looks deep within the hearts of a men and women and he studies their motives and thoughts. God is putting nations in their place to let them seek the only one who can help them. It is hard to find sincerity because most of humankind is lying to them-selves first of all to their own hearts content. Most men and women have not experienced the eternal presence of Jehovah.

There are floods, earth-quakes and wild fire all over the world where people are losing homes and their lives. When a nation is disobedient God will send famine, disease and war. All these are becoming to be a threat to our world today. Sin came into the world and brought with it the curse. Sin is separation from God and it changed the atmosphere toward man and the earth. It brings wrath instead of the love that God has for all Humankind.

God's Holy Spirit in a believer helps change the atmosphere and environment. Evil men want to do right, but lack the wisdom and strength of God to perform it. It is urgent to know the sins that lurks in their hearts because they will not look in the mirror of the word to see their inner blemishes and filthiness of their heart.

"The Lord by wisdom hath founded the earth, by understanding hath he established the heavens" Proverbs 3:19. Humankind has become its own worst enemy. Environmental terrorist is an act of violence committed in support of environmental causes against people or property. Environmental terrorism consists of one or more unlawful acts that harm and destroy environmental resources and deprive others of their use. Example; Our government is running oil pipes thru neighborhoods that spill and mix with drinking water accidently.

There is Deep Ecology that is an environmental philosophy that promotes the inherent worth of all living beings regardless of their instrumental utility to human needs. The world is re-structioning modern human societies in accordance with such ideas. The curse of the Lord is in the house of the wicked: but he blesseth the habitation of the just. Eco Feminism the study or philosophy of how there is a connection between women and nature. This is how nature and women are treated by the patriarchal society.

Social ecology is the study of living things and there habitat. Bio-regionalism, is a philosophy that suggest that political, cultural, and economic systems are more sustainable and just if they are organized around naturally defined areas called bioregions. Eco terrorism is a form of radical environmentalism that arose out of the school of thought that brought all these about.

The recycling and extracting of metal waste using non- toxic bacteria has become another issue. Money and greed again is the motivation. Man has tunnel vision by not being able to see no further than their greed and the dollar. God's wisdom will show you the end from the beginning.

Precious metals such as 15% of gold and silver found in high tech goods are recovered from cell phones, tablets, computers and other electronic or electrical devices. There is over 21 billion dollars worth of gold and silver found in this waste. It has been said that one man's trash is another man's treasure.

Proverbs 3:13-14, says, "Happy is the man that findeth wisdom, and the man that getteth understanding. (Vs.14), "For the merchandise of it is better than the merchandise of silver, and the gain thereof than fine gold." Wisdom is more precious than all you can desire and nothing can be compared to it. When you get wisdom you get long life and riches and honor.

After the usable life of these electronics they become waste, however less than 15% of these precious metals deposited are recovered for reuse. The rest is left in the waste pile creating potential health and environmental hazards. I stated in my earlier book how plastic bags being a hazard in our oceans and seas. Prices are rising across the board. The price of gold is rising per ounce to 5 times as much.

Let me remind you what to get. Wisdom is the principle thing; therefore get wisdom: and with all thy getting get understanding." "Businesses must recover what they can to continue their quest of manufacturing of these products said, Dr. Ruedige-Kuehr, Executive Secretary of Solving the E-Waste Problem. When the word of the Lord becomes a reproach they have no delight in it because it goes against humankind's plans. Jeremiah 6:19 tells us to, "Hear, O earth: behold, I will bring evil upon this people, even the fruit of their thoughts, because they have not hearkened unto my words, nor to my law, but rejected it."

CHAPTER 4

KEEP YOUR FOCUS ON GOD

God's word warns us of our hidden faults that make us yield to do wrong. Repentance keeps our mind clear of guilt. We should have a desire to please God thru our words and thoughts. Psalms 19:14 says, "May the words of my mouth and the meditation of my heart be pleasing to you, O Lord, my rock, my redeemer."

We serve God because of the benefits that we receive in Psalms 103. God forgives our iniquities and heal our diseases. We should serve God because he is God. We should seek eternal life because all the wealth in the world is not enough to buy one soul and keep it from everlasting hell. Those who fight against God will end in hell fire burning always and never ending. God gave his creation a choice but some did not listen instead they are like the waves of the sea tossed to and fro.

They don't even want God around them. So God let them go their way to go after their own blind and stubborn desires. They have no fear of Jehovah and reject the wisdom that he gives to his creation. They are their own God and they have limited knowledge about themselves and the world. Humankind is feeling its way through experiments while making mistake after mistake causing many lives to be lost.

They become a curse and everything they do fail until they learn to fear God and realize that Jehovah is in supreme charge of all the earth. In the book of Judges in chapter 2:10 reminds me of the generation of today. When the baby boomers die off then most of the Millennium generation will not be worshipping Jehovah as God.

Their own iniquities shall take control of them and they will be bound by the cords of their sins. This is that generation of gangs that, Proverbs 6:13, "He winketh with his eyes, he speaketh with his feet, he teaches with his fingers." They are not caring about God and his mighty miracles but there will always be those who worship God Jehovah. There are many people caught in traps and snares today because of dealings with evil people over the internet. The Holy Scriptures tells us in the book of Proverbs 23:7, "For as he thinketh in his heart, so is he: Eat and drink, saith he to thee; but his heart is not with thee."

Jesus Christ is like a bad taste in the mouths of those who are ignorant about him. When a man dies he will be away from God's presence because sin is separation from God. There are those who run, duck and hide from God all their lives. One day their evasive tactics will run out and they will have to face God in one of these two ways. They will meet Jesus Christ as Lord, or they are going to meet him as judge, but they are going to meet him.

They worship their sin gods that brings the curse instead of giving God the glory honor and the praise for the air they are breathing. People are selling their souls to the devil at a fast rate for only a moment of pleasure and they don't even get the whole moment. Satan steals their future and destroys their lives or they are killed during the process of their sin. Only God's word can make the dead live again and speak of future events with as much certainty as though they were already past.

Problems and trials in life help us learn patience. Patience develops strength of character in us and helps us trust God more. When we continue in patience we become strong and steady in the Lord and the power of His might. Then the love of God is shed abroad in our hearts by the Holy Spirit and his love abides in us richly. "But God showed his great love for us by sending Christ to die for us while we were still sinners" (Romans 5:8 LB).

Our nation is on a mission to fight against God and his word. In 2 Chronicles 36:15-16 LB shows us how "Jehovah the God of their fathers sent his prophets again and again to warn them, for he had compassion on his people and on his Temple. (Vs.16), "But the people mocked these messengers of God and despised their words, scoffing at the prophets until the anger of the Lord could no longer be restrained, and there was no longer any remedy."

God can use America's enemy to destroy us completely, God forbid. Repent by having remorse for your sins every one of you and be baptized in the name of Jesus Christ for the remission of sin and receive the gift of the Holy Spirit.

God gave us the Ten Commandments to show us how far we were from obeying him. Because of Adam's sin brought punishment to all and sin ruled over all men and brought us to death and the curse. Now God kindness came to us by Jesus Christ by his obedience and put us in right standing with God resulting in eternal life and blessings.

When you got saved your evil desires were nailed to the cross with Jesus Christ so that your sin-loving body would lose its control. Sin was knocked down for the count and it is up to each individual not to let sin get up in their lives. Keep sin and the devil down on the mat knocked out and unresponsive and don't give in to its desires.

Give yourself completely to God. Stop being the victim and stay the victor with the victory in Jesus Christ. With Jesus Christ you are free and under God's favor and mercy. We should know that at any time you can choose your own master because Jehovah gave us the ability to choose. You can choose Satan that brings sin and the curse unto death or Jesus Christ in obedience unto him for righteousness. Let me remind you that "to whom ye yield yourselves servants to obey his servant ye are to whom you obey; whether sin unto death or obedience unto righteousness."

If you sin, repent of that sin with a sincere heart! Admit it, quit it and get back with it, get back in line with the word of God. We must keep programming and reprogramming ourselves in God's word. Do this so you can be right with God and receive his benefits that include holiness and everlasting life.

When you were baptized you rose again with Christ. You resembled his death, burial and resurrection. You came up out of the water and became a new person as Christ did when he came out of the water he received the Holy Spirit. We must read our Holy Scriptures so that we can resemble Jesus Christ as much as we can. When we arise from the dead as Jesus Christ did our bodies will be like His from terrestrial (earthy) to celestial (heavenly or spiritual). He came and was baptized and gave us a perfect example of how to be Christ-like.

We have to ask God for his Holy Spirit and tarry until it comes. The Holy Spirit can lead and guide you on your journey with Jesus Christ. The spirit led him into the wilderness to be tempted. With God working in us by the Holy Spirit and it gives us the power of God.

At first Satan was working in you when you were his slave in bondage and in chains living in his dungeons and pigpens. You lived a sloppy life. Your sin aroused all kinds of evil and forbidden desires in you. Now you are going thru the process of becoming a new creature. So keep working towards that day when you will finally be all that Jesus Christ saved you for and wants you to be.

Regardless of your pass, strain to reach the end of the race, and receive the prize for which God is calling you up to heaven, because of what Christ Jesus did for you. If you drop the ball remember you can recover it just by "Repentance" with a sincere heart.

When you were in sin you even thought you were doing right because you did not understand God's law. Now you know that sin was trying to take you out and made you guilty of death. As one of the malefactors in Mathew 23 said to the other on the cross does thou not fear God? There are people faithful to sin unto death even as Jesus Christ was faithful in righteousness unto death. The other two men on each side of Jesus on the cross were getting their just reward, condemnation for their deeds but Jesus had done nothing wrong.

God gave us an inside out overhaul by placing his spirit on the inside of us when we got saved so we could follow the Holy Spirit inside of us. This was the same spirit that fell on Jesus Christ after he came out of the water from being baptized. When he walked the earth he was our comforter but after leaving earth he sent us another comforter called the Holy Ghost. The Holy Spirit leads to life and peace.

That old sinful nature will never obey God and it never will. You must have the Holy Spirit inside you to be in Christ. Because of sin your body will die but your spirit will live forever obeying God to heaven or condemned by sin in hell. Obedience to Jehovah will get you to heaven. Disobedience to God gives you a one way ticket to hell.

You can only choose while you live because five minutes after you die is too late. When you repent of your sin Christ has pardoned it. He forgives you and then you must learn to forgive yourself. Romans 8:11 LB says, "And if the Spirit of God, who raised up Jesus from the dead, is in you, he will make your dying bodies live again after you die, by means of this same Holy Spirit." We are saved by trusting for something that we don't yet have. We receive what Jesus Christ has done for us by faith and everlasting life upon His return.

We must remember that "If God be for us who can be against us"? Be the smart man or women that you think you are and choose Jesus Christ. He will be your Lord while you live or die and he has already defeated death. "Either way, you can't get away from him living or dead."

It will be heaven or hell. You are going to meet him as Lord or you are going to meet him as judge but you are going to meet him. Psalms 90:7 "For we are consumed by thine anger, and by thy wrath are we troubled." In (Vs.12), we ask God, "So teach us to number our days, that we may apply our hearts unto wisdom."

Each of us will give an account of himself to God. So let your work appear unto us and establish the work of our hands Lord God. Lord God you make me glad to do your work and make me win with the great works of your hands coming from your deep thoughts. Don't do anything that will cause criticism against yourself even though you know that what you do is right. "Let not then your good be evil spoken of"" Romans 14:16 KJV.

Romans 14:16 LB. "In this situation, happy is the man who does not sin by doing what he knows is right." Remember that the carnal mind is the enmity against God and we should be led by the spirit of God. Psalms 24:1 tells us that "The earth is the Lord's and the fullness thereof; the world, and they that dwell therein." We are God's property invaded by sin from Satan. "While it is said, To- day if ye will hear his voice, harden not your heart, as in the provocation" Hebrews 3:15. Stop making people annoyed and angry instead help them by sharing the light inside you.

Psalms 90:1-2 says, "Lord thou hast been our dwelling place in all generations." (Vs.2), "Before the mountains were brought forth, or ever thou hadst formed the earth and the world, even from everlasting to everlasting, thou art God." God's throne is from everlasting. "Thy throne is established of old: thou art from everlasting" Psalms 93:2.

Romans 16:25-27LB, "I commit you to God, who is able to make you strong and steady in the Lord, just as the Gospel say, and just as I have told you. This is God's salvation for you Gentiles, kept secret from the beginning of time. But now as the prophets foretold and as God commands, this message is being preach every -where, so that people all around the world will have faith in Christ and obey him. To God, who alone is wise, be the glory forever through Jesus Christ our Lord."

So I do not worry, fret, or have anxiety about anything, I do not have a care," (Philippians 4:6; 1Peter 5:6,7). The God of peace will soon crush Satan under our feet. God's plan for our lives was hid in former times before the world began, and the wise men of this world understood it not. If they did they would have never crucified Jesus Christ. God gave us his spirit to show us all his deepest secrets. God knows how to make the garden grow in your hearts. He does this for us so we can have his thoughts and mind. God uses the wisdom of this world and man's own brilliance to trap him. He stumbles over his own wisdom and falls.

God gave us the whole world to use and he gave us life and death as our servants. John 3:16 "For God so loved the world, that He gave His only begotten Son, that whosoever believeth in him should not perish, but have everlasting life." Don't look back because we have the present now and the future to come. We may look good on the outside but when the Lord returns he will show us what we really look like on the inside of our hearts. To get the knowledge of God to open up to us we must truly love God. We must know that there is one God and no other and that is the Lord Jesus Christ who made everything and gives us life. God gave us lessons to warn us not to desire evil things and worship idols eating and drinking to them. God is our mighty Rock of spiritual refreshment.

Reading the word of God showed me where 23,000 fell dead in one day for sinning by fornicators committing sexual immorality in 1 Corinthians 10:8. One of the fruit of the spirit is patience. Sin is dangerous and we don't want to try God's patience when your cup of sin becomes full. We don't want to see God's anger when his "Popeye" comes out and he says, "I took all I can stand and I can't stand no more."

Jehovah do not like murmuring and complaining from those who are ungrateful. This is just a few examples of things that happened to Israel as objects lessons to warn us against doing the same things. They were written down so we could read about them and learn about them to remind us in these last days as our world near it's end 1Corinthians 10:4-11 LB Paraphrase. Those who think they have it all together need to "take heed lest he fall."

We should know that no temptation is irresistible and none of us is exempt from sin. God always gives us a way of escape from every sin. 1 Corinthians 10:21KJV, "Ye cannot drink the cup of the Lord and the cup of devils, ye cannot be partakers of the Lord's table and of the table of devils." The Lord's plan for men and women was laid out before the beginning of this earth. The Holy Bible says in 1Corithians11:10-11 L B, "So if a woman should wear a covering on her head as a sign that she is under man's authority, a fact for all the angels to notice and rejoice in". (Vs.11), "But remember that in God's plan men and women need each other. For although the first woman came out of man, all men have been born from women ever since, and both men and women come from God."

The God inspired Word teaches us and gives us instructions and reproofs to lead us on our journey in Christ Jesus. God's word is not the author of confusion because it is the same yesterday, today and forever. It is the unadulterated, uncompromising, unchanging word of God. How can it be unadulterated when you read it if you are committing adultery?

It is unadulterated in 1Peter 1:23 'Having been born again, not of corruptible seed, but incorruptible, through the word of God, which lives and remains forever." It is unchanging and we hold on to in worship and holding on to his unchanging word by reading it, talking about it, memorizing it and meditating on it. It is uncompromising by making no adjustments of difference, making no concessions. And it is inaccessible to flexible bargaining and have an unyielding an uncompromising attitude.

There are too many goats bucking in leadership positions in our society and God's church. Our love should be to God whose air we breathe and our deliverer. 1 Corinthians 13:7 LB "If you love someone you will be loyal to him no matter what the cost. You will always believe in him, always expect the best of him, and always stand your ground in defending him." So my dear brothers, since future victory is sure, be strong and steady, always abounding in the Lord's work, for you know that nothing you do for the Lord is ever wasted as it would be if there were no resurrection." "And whatsoever you do in word or deed, do all in the name of the Lord Jesus, giving thanks to God and the Father by him" Colossians 3:17.

God wants to send his special blessing that you find in Numbers 6:24-26. "Now the Lord told Moses tell Aaron and his sons that they are to give this special blessing to the people of Israel: "May the Lord bless and protect you; may the Lord's face radiate with joy because of you, may he be gracious to you, show you his favor, and give you his peace. This is how we call down God's blessings and God said he will personally bless them. We should always be at home in the Lord.

The addiction of sin reminds me of Balaam and Balak and we should say only what God tell you to say. Satan tempted Jesus and Jesus told him what was written. Balak told Balaam that he would promote him to great honor. Balak tried to blame God. The earth is the Lord and the fullness thereof and all that dwell therein. Balak said the Lord has kept you from it. We must trust in the Lord with all thine heart and lean not unto thine own understanding, In all thy ways acknowledge him, and he shall direct thy paths" (Vs.7), Be not wise in thine own eyes: fear the Lord, and depart from evil" Proverbs 3:5-6-7.

Balaam knew "If any of you lacks wisdom, let him ask of God, "that giveth to all men liberally and upbraided not: and it shall be given him." Satan even told Jesus he would give him all the kingdoms if he would bow and worship him knowing Jesus created it all. That block buster Satan will say anything to you to advance his kingdom. You better look out and remember the greater one lives in you.

CHAPTER 5

LIVE A REPENTANT LIFESTYLE

The pull of sin is so strong and it will test your love for God. None of us should deliberately place ourselves in a position to be tempted. Every time you step into the bright lights of a casino Satan is showing you all the kingdoms of the world. We must have a feeling or showing regret for the things we do against God. When we do what is right in the eyes of the Lord all will go well with us and our children. We all become what we think by forming habits. Be careful about what you think and guard your heart because from the abundance of the heart the mouth speaks and the issues of life flows from our heart.

Disobedience brings the curse. Your words affect you and those around you when you speak the curse instead of the blessing. When you are living in sin you are walking in the curse. You can rebel against God for only so long before he forsakes you. In 2 Chronicles 15:2 says, "The Lord is with you while you are with Him, If you seek him he will be found by you, but if you forsake him he will forsake you."

Remember in Deuteronomy 28:20-22 LB "For the Lord himself will send his personal curse upon you. You will be confused and a failure in everything you do, until at last you are destroyed because of the sin of forsaking him. (Vs.21) "He will send disease among you until you are destroyed from the face of the land which you are about to possess. (Vs.22) "He will send tuberculosis, fever, infections, plague, and war. He will blight your crops, covering them with mildew. All these devastations shall pursue you until you perish."

We must live a repentant life style. When you sin hurry-up and repent. Get that off you fast, quick and in a hurry before you become complacent in that sin. Hurry before guilt, shame and condemnation set in and your sin catches up with you and you start to reap the sin you have been sowing.

God has a contract with humankind in Deuteronomy 29:1 thru Deuteronomy 29:29 where the Lord commanded Moses to give His words of the covenant to the children of Israel. The secret thing belongs to the Lord. Curses come when humankind breaks that contract with God and when they walk in their own stubborn ways. Ask God to show me the path to walk in and to point out the right road for me to walk. Guide me clearly the path you want me to travel. When man realizes that their deeds are known they become frighten. No man or woman committing a crime wants to be known. Lawbreakers of God today actually believe they are right to fight against God whose air they are breathing.

Magicians and Sorcerers were using Secret Arts when Moses and Aaron went before Pharaoh casting their rod like a snake doing the signs that God had given them. Just as the people are today they are unimpressed with the messengers that God sends until death. Satan's counterfeiter's copied God's ministers and every time God was respite giving him (Pharoah) a suspended sentence. God is letting their heart harden. The finger of God speaks loud to them in Exodus 8:19. In chapter 12:30 when there was a great cry in Egypt. God will make you scream to him as he breaks your pride down to the lowest denominator.

As long as trouble is near people want to be delivered. As soon as they are delivered they run back to their troubled slop pins and vomit that God delivered them from. Their hearts are hardened in their stubbornness and refuse to listen. All those who have no regard for Jehovah and his word will be left in the storms of life. They refuse to submit to God. Sometimes trouble gets too hard for evil people and it drives them to repentance.

They are like Pharaoh when Moses told him to let God's people go until the death angel appeared. Even when death comes close to some still will not submit to God or any kind of authority. They only submit to the penal system and death. Both of them are forms of death. The penal systems death is written on paper when they are moved out of population. They end up dying in their sin if not repented of. God will bring you out of your captivity if you repent and turn from your sins to him with a sincere heart.

Prayer: Ephesians 3:14-21 "For this cause I bow my knees unto the Father of our Lord Jesus Christ, Of whom the whole family in heaven and earth is named, That he would grant you (me), according to the riches of his glory, to be strengthen with might by his Spirit in the inner man; That Christ may dwell in your (my) hearts by faith; that ye, (I may be) being rooted and grounded in love, May be able to comprehend with all saints what is the breadth, length, and depth, and height; And to know the love of Christ, which passeth knowledge, that ye (I) might be filled with all the fullness of God. Now unto him that is able to do exceeding abundantly above all that we ask or think, according to the power that worketh in us (me), Unto him be glory in the church by Christ Jesus throughout all ages, world without end. Amen.

CHAPTER 6

UNDERSTANDING JESUS AS GOD

We all need the assurance of understanding about God to be able to acknowledge the mystery of God and of the Father, and of Christ from eternity to eternity. This is where all the treasures of wisdom and knowledge are hidden. Don't let those who philosophy lead you away from Christ into believing the traditions of men because in Christ lay all the fullness of the Godhead bodily. Jesus Christ put on flesh to show us how to walk in the power of the spirit. He is the Father of spirits and we are complete in him and our life is hid within God. Jesus Christ is all, in all, and all in it.

Jesus Christ in the book of Colossians 1:15-18 "Who is the image of the invisible God, the firstborn of every creature: (Vs.16) "For by him were all things created, that are in heaven, and that are in earth, visible and invisible, whether they be thrones, or dominion, or principalities, or powers: all things were created by him and for him: (Vs.17), "And he is before all things, and by him all things consist. (Vs.18), "And he is the head of the body, the church: who is the beginning, the firstborn from the dead; that in all things he might have the preeminence." In Vs.20 "And, having made peace through the blood of his cross, by him to reconcile all things unto himself; by him, I say, whether they be things in earth, or things in heaven."

People want what God has but they don't want Jesus Christ. They don't want Jesus Christ because they don't know who he is in the flesh. "My people are destroyed for lack of knowledge" Hosea 4:6. The ox knoweth his owner and the ass his masters crib: but Israel doth not know, my people doth not consider" Isaiah 1:3. Satan knew God's power because Pharaoh in all his wickedness ask Moses for a blessing when he was leading Israel on their way out of Egypt. Yes, demons believe and tremble. When we are punished by the Lord it is so we will not be condemned with the rest of the world.

God wants to reason with you. He said in Isaiah 1:19-20, "If ye be willing and obedient, ye shall eat the good of the land: (Vs.20), "But if ye refuse and rebel, ye shall be devoured with the sword: for the mouth of the Lord hath spoken it." Israel or the churches are going away backward. God is saying who required this at your hand, to tread my courts? It is iniquity even the solemn meeting. There are people in the world that claim to be inspired by God's Spirit and turn right around and curse Jesus Christ with their mouth. They don't know who he was when he walked this earth and don't know how he can be in them.

There are some people that have fellowship with the Father and not the Son. "This then is the message which we have heard of him, and declare unto you, that God is light and in him is no darkness at all" 1 John 1:5. Sometimes I would pray in the barber shop and every time that I would say in the name of Jesus Christ a few would say you were doing good until you said that name. I would say, what name? Jesus Christ! I guess it was making the demon inside them tremble.

They did not know Jesus Christ the one from before the beginning of time. Jesus is from everlasting to everlasting. I ask them to spell Jesus and they could not. The world and the things of the world such as the lust of the flesh, the lust of the eyes and the pride of life was their subjects. 1 John 2:19, says, "They went out from us, but they were not of us; for if they had been of us, they would no doubt have continued with us: but they went out, that they might be made manifest that they were not all of us."

I would say to them, why can't you say Jesus? They could not. You can say that Jesus Christ is Lord if you have his Spirit inside you. I said to them what do you have against the man who had the Spirit of God in him who raised the dead, and made the blind see? He came to put us back in right standing with our creator. 1 John 3:5, "And ye know that he was manifested to take away our sins, and in him is no sin." In Vs.8 "He that commiteth sin is of the devil; for the devil sinneth from the beginning. For this purpose the Son of God was manifested, that he might destroy the works of the devil."

Verse 10 in 1 John chapter 3 says, "In this the children of God are manifest, and the children of the devil: whosoever doeth not righteousness is not of God, neither he that loveth not his brother." The men at the barber shop were the ones that wanted what God has but they don't want God's Son. They did not know that Jesus the man had God's Spirit that hovered over the water from the beginning in him. God is Spirit and his Spirit fell upon him like a dove on the man that was born from Mary after he was baptized by John the Baptiser. Jesus was born to be our sacrifice for the sins of the world. God searched and could not find any man worthy.

In the book of John 1:1-5 Living Bible, "Before Anything Else existed, there was Christ, with God. "He has always been alive and is himself God. (Vs.3), "He created everything there is—nothing exist that he didn't make. (Vs.4), "Eternal life is in him, and this life gives light to all mankind. (Vs.5), "His life is the light that shines through the darkness and the darkness can never extinguish it." In the book of John 1:1 Jesus Christ is that "In the beginning was the Word and the Word was with God, and the Word was God." Jesus Christ is that one God, and one Lord. He is Lord of lords.

John the Baptist said in John 1:30, "He is the one I was talking about when I said, Soon a man far greater than I am is coming, who existed long before me." Isaiah 9:6 in The New Living Translation tells us about Jesus Christ, "For a child is born to us, but God have never been a child. "A son is given to us." God needed flesh for his sacrifice and made Jesus in Mary. Isaiah 7:14 says, "Therefore the Lord himself shall give you a sign; Behold, a virgin shall conceive, and bear a son, and shall call his name Immanuel I is the translation of the original Hebrew word which comes from Immanuel. Emanuel with the E is the translation from the Greek word "Emmanouel" because New Testament was written in Greek original transcript spell Emmanuel with an E in Mathew 1:23 King James Version. The name means God with us. The child grew in statue and years. God don't need to grow and he is timeless with no birthday. God's spirit came into Mary and then Jesus after he was baptized by John the Baptist.

The government will rest on his shoulders. And he will be called: Wonderful Counselor, Mighty God, Eternal Father, Prince of Peace" (Isaiah 9:6LB). Jesus is all that God's word says He is. In Mathew 1:23 "Behold the virgin shall conceive and bear a son, and they shall call his name "Emmanuel" which means, God with us". God never had a mother and flesh and blood is not in heaven. God is bigger than the universe. God is spirit he is neither black nor white. Numbers 23:19, "God is not a man, that he should lie; neither the son of a man, that he should repent: hath he said, and shall he not do it? Or hath he spoken, and shall he not make it good? God got in that man and functioned thru that man to show us how to walk in his spirit. Conversely, this scripture is telling us that man will lie just because his mouth is moving.

In the book of Isaiah 9:6 shows us that Jesus name is from everlasting. Before Mary and Joseph was born Jesus the Christ was already here and prophesied in the book of Isaiah. Isaiah 9:6 says "For unto us a child is born, unto us a son is given: and the government shall be upon his shoulders: and his name shall be called Wonderful, Counsellor, The mighty God, The everlasting Father, The Prince of Peace." Adam's figure was of the similitude of him to come. Jesus is the Son of God and is called the second Adam. 1 John 3:1 reveals, "Behold, what manner of love the Father hath bestowed upon us, that we should be called the sons of God: therefore the world knoweth us not, because it knew him not." When Jesus Christ return we will be like him and we will see him as he is.

Jesus was predestined. We know that Jesus abides in us by the Spirit which he hath given us called the Holy Spirit. We can't believe every spirit and we must try the spirits whether they are of God because there are those who confess that Jesus Christ did not come in the flesh and he is called the antichrist. Jesus had a nature of spirit and a nature of flesh.

Jesus the man ate, slept, grew, and was taught by God's spirit who is the Father of Spirits. He always gave the Father the credit.

The spirit the water and blood was designed to work together that came out of Jesus Christ on the Cross. Blood and water came out when he was speared in the side. Blood and water is the natural. Jesus flesh and bones went to the tomb. The only thing left was spirit that came out when he cried out and gave up the ghost or spirit. The spirit came out with a loud voice crying out to a spirit larger than himself saying, in Mathew 27:46, "And about the ninth hour Jesus the flesh cried with a loud voice, saying, Eli, Eli, la-ma sa-bach'-tha-ni? That is to say, My God, my God, why hast thou forsaken me?

After crying out a second time he gave up the Ghost or the spirit. His spirit went to the lower parts of the earth where he preached to the spirits in prison three days because he was the Father of spirits. He took the keys of death and Hades for himself. He was the first begotten of the dead. When blood was in Jesus he was called natural because the life of the flesh is the blood. When he went back into the body in the grave he got in that body it became spiritual or celestial.

He got in the same body that Mary had birth him. In 1 Corinthians 15:44, It was now called an It. "It was sown a natural body and raise a spiritual body." Jesus spirit came from God and went back to God after he was glorified. After returning to the body in the tomb and the spirit quickening the dead his body walked thru walls as he preached to his disciples opening their understanding to the scriptures. He was now spiritual. The spirit that fell on Jesus after his baptism came from God and after opening the disciples understanding went back to the Father.

In Revelation 1:18 Jesus says, I am the Living One; I was dead, and now look, I am alive forever and ever! And I hold the keys of death and Hades. This means he having the keys of death is now a risen Christ that has control and authority over death. In John10:17-18, where he says, I lay down my life and only to take it up again. He said I have authority to lay it down and authority to take it up again. In Revelation 9:1-2 an angel is given a key to control over, the bottomless pit, and he uses it to open that pit. Later an angel is seen locking things in the bottomless pit in Rev 20:1-2. God gave believers the power to bind and loose in Mathew 16:19.

Our bodies will do the same at the resurrection. 1 Thessalonians 4:14 tells us, "For if we believe that Jesus died and rose again, even so them also which sleep in Jesus will God bring with him." It is raised incorruptible. It is corruptible putting on incorruption. It is the mortal that must put on immortality. 1 Corinthians 15:51-52 says, "Behold, I shew you a mystery: We shall not all sleep, but we shall all be changed, (Vs.52), "In a moment, in the twinkling of an eye, at the last trump: for the trumpet shall sound, and the dead shall be raised incorruptible, and we shall all be changed." The body that we plant in the grave will not be the body that will be quickened, because the body that is quicken will be greater than the body that went in the grave when it is raised.

Our body takes on the spirit making it animated and functions as natural. The body is dead without the spirit. This is an inside out job. God's spirit got in the natural body of Jesus that did the works and this he told the disciples that the Holy Spirit will also be in you. This was the example of how God's perfect plan for imperfect people plays out. God hid himself in our body because he is a God that hides himself.

Isaiah 45:15ESV, "Truly you are a God that hides himself. KJV "Verily thou art a God that hidest thyself, O God of Israel, the Savior." God hid himself in Mary and she became pregnant. Mary birth flesh and blood and God's spirit hid himself in Jesus after he grew in statue and years. The Holy Spirit got in that body after Jesus baptism the same way it will fall on us when we repent and is baptized in the name of Jesus Christ ask and expecting to receive it. The doctrine of baptism with water was for the body and flesh. The spirit, blood and water are elements of the New Birth.

The baptism of the Holy Spirit was to be baptized with spirit and fire. The Holy Spirit burns out everything that is not of God. The doctrine of baptism of water, spirit and the covering of the blood of Jesus Christ is the knowledge of the new birth. The doctrine of God in 1st Timothy 1:1 says, "Paul, an apostle of Jesus Christ by the commandment of God our Savior, and Lord Jesus Christ which is our hope." 1Timothy

2:5 says, "For there is one God, and one mediator between God and men, the man Jesus Christ."

Jesus is our Savior and Just God, Great God, Almighty God. God was in Jesus and Christ is the title and the anointing of God. Jesus is from everlasting and he was that God in the man Jesus Christ the anointed one. Isaiah 35:4-7. God is a God that hides himself, God hid himself in THE BODY of Jesus. "For God so loved the world he gave his only begotten Son." God made the body of Jesus in Mary and afterwards got in that body. God is spirit and placed himself in Jesus. Jesus Christ is Lord of Lord. One lord human and the other lord spirit Lord Jesus. Jesus said my Father is greater than I. God gave Jesus his Holy Spirit and power and was manifested in Jesus the man. Jesus said the Father that dwelleth in me, he doeth the work.

Dig deep into the wisdom of God and he will help you understand the mystery of Christ. We serve God by the spirit that dwelleth in us. Jesus flesh never took the credit. He always pointed to the Father. Great is the Mystery of God. 1Timothy 3:16, "And without controversy great is the mystery of godliness; God was manifested in the flesh, justified in the Spirit, seen of angels, preached unto the Gentiles, believed on in the world, received up into glory." "God is not a man that he should lie in Numbers 23:19. The form of Jesus in the flesh took on the form of God by God's spirit in him making him in the image of God. Jesus said if you don't believe me at least believe the works that I do. Jesus made flesh and blood who will publish the word of the Lord. Ephesians 2:15 shows us God's design was to unite the two sections of humanity spirit and flesh in Himself so as to form one new man.

Jesus name was inherited. Hebrews 1;4 reveals to us that, "Being made so much better than the angels, as he hath by inheritance obtained a more excellent name than they." Philippians 2:5, 6, 7, 8, 9-10. (Vs.5)"Let this mind be in you which was also in Christ Jesus. (Vs.6), "Who, being in the form of God, thought it not robbery to be equal with God; (Vs.7), "But made himself of no reputation, and took upon him the form of a servant and was made in the likeness of men. (Vs.8), "And being found in the fashion as a man, he humbled himself, and became obedient unto death, even the death of the cross. (Vs.9), "Wherefore God also hath highly exalted him, and given him a name which is above every name (Vs.10), (Vs.10)"That at the name of Jesus every knee should bow, of things in heaven, and things in earth, and things under the earth. Even the dead and demons have to obey that name.

In Titus1:2 "In hope of eternal life, which God, that cannot lie, promised before the world began." Jesus Christ was God by the Spirit of God that descended on him like a dove. God is spirit. God's spirit got into the man Jesus to show us by example how to walk in His spirit in us. There is only one God. Isaiah 45:21"Tell ye, and bring them near; yea, let them take counsel together: who hath declared this from ancient time? Who hath told it from that time? Have not I the Lord? And there is no God beside me; a just God and a Savior; there is none beside me." We must come into the knowledge of the new birth.

John the Baptist said, I indeed baptize you with water unto repentance: but he that cometh after me is mightier than I, whose shoes I am not worthy to bear: he shall baptize you with the Holy Ghost, and with fire." We need the Holy Ghost to burn out everything that is not of God.

Jesus Christ was also with Moses in the book of (1Corithians 10:1-4 KJV),"Moreover, brethren, I would not that ye should be ignorant, how that all our fathers were under the cloud, and all passed through the sea; (Vs.2),"And were all baptized unto Moses in the cloud and in the sea; (Vs.3), "And did all eat the same spiritual meat; "And did all drink the same spiritual drink: for they drank of that spiritual Rock that followed them: and that Rock was Christ."

Jesus Christ was talking to God in John 17:4-5LB saying, "I brought glory to you here on earth by doing everything you told me to. "And now Father, reveal my glory as I stand in your presence, the glory we shared before the world began". Jesus prayed to God that "I have given them the glory you gave me—the glorious unity of being one, as we are. He continued in Vs. 24, "You gave me the glory because you loved me before the world began."

There are those who still want the Father without the Son and that is not happening. The Holy Bible says in 1 Corinthians 12:3LB, "So I want you to know that no one speaking by the Spirit of God will curse

Jesus, and no one can say Jesus is Lord except by the Holy Spirit." This let me know what work had to be done in the barber shop.

People are alright with Jehovah God but the name of Jesus Christ put a bad taste in their mouth. They wanted only to believe God but none of them wanted Jesus Christ or even knew who he was. There are some who don't believe in the New Testament. There are some who think the Old Testament is outdated. They reject the whole counsel of God. Jesus Christ was the Spirit or anointing that fell upon the prophets all through the Old Testament. God want us to eat the whole book of the Holy Scriptures.

Jesus Christ is the Holy Spirit that fell in the upper room. He was that another comforter. John 14:16-18 says, 'I will pray the Father, and he will give you another helper, that he may abide with you forever (Vs.17), "the spirit of truth, whom the world cannot receive, because it neither sees Him nor knows Him, for He dwells with you and will be in you. (Vs.18), "I will not leave you as orphans, I will come to you."

This shows us that he is the Holy Spirit. John 14:26 says, "But the comforter which is the Holy Ghost, whom the Father will send in my name, he shall teach you all things and bring all things to your remembrance." John 4:24 "God is Spirit and they that worship him must worship him in spirit and in truth. That spirit got in the man Jesus giving him the anointing and that anointing is Christ and the God who is spirit sent His spirit back to us as helper. Jesus said that we would do greater works than his.

We must keep good records. So I had to go to "The Record." 1 John 5:11-13KJV, "And this is the record, that God hath given to us eternal life, and this life is in his Son. (Vs.12) "He that hath the Son hath life, and he that hath not the Son of God hath not life." (Vs. 1),"These things have I written unto you that believe on the name of the Son of God; that ye may know that ye have eternal life, and that ye may believe on the name of the Son of God" Read 1 John 5 from Vs. 1to 21 again and again and don't let this truth get pass you. Be sure that your soul is not wrong at death.

Too much focus is on the preacher and not on God and his word. The people in the barber shop were talking about something they heard and would not read for themselves. They love worshipping the good things in life other than God who made the good things. We all must learn as God perfects that which concerns us. Stay far from evil places of darkness but instead be a light in that dark place and expose their shame. They love darkness to hide their sin. They are the walking dead and God want you to slap them with His word to wake them up from their sleep. Be careful as you watch and pray in these last days. We must buy up every opportunity to bless God.

There are many evils when you hang out with drunkards. Let the Holy Spirit lead and guide you not the spirits you get from drugs and alcohol contrary to God's word. Sing praises and let the Joy of the Lord be your strength as you thank him always. Your strength comes from God's mighty power from within you. Dress up by putting on Christ every morning. "For we are not fighting against people made of flesh and blood, but against persons without bodies-- We are fighting "the evil rulers of the unseen world. They are "those mighty satanic beings and great evil princes of darkness who rule this world; and against huge numbers of wicked spirits in the spirit world" Ephesians 6:12 LB.

Be ready for all who are immoral and impure those who contradict the Good News of our blessed God. They love to disobey their conscience and deliberately do wrong. Don't let the love of money change you and make you fight against him who has it all. God says in Haggai 2:8 "The silver is mine and the gold is mine, saith the Lord of host". When you are on your money quest you will run into all kinds of temptations. The sin that you commit will bring to you many sorrows believe me. Rape and fornication are only a moment of pleasure that can last a life time in the penitentiary. What is so bad about it is that you don't even get the whole moment.

Jesus Christ died to relieve us of the guilt of our sin sickness by repentance to relieve our minds. God delights in our obedience. There is no sacrifice that we can make to God better than obedience. Hebrews 10:14 "For by one offering he made forever perfect in the sight of God all those whom he is making holy." Then he wrote his laws in their minds and heart so when we repent he will never again remember our sins. Our sins are forgiven and forgotten. Christ renewed our relationship with God and tore down the curtain between God and man never to use the blood sacrifice of bull and goats again.

Satan worshippers still use the blood of animal sacrifice in their temples across America. What! Satan has temples in America and ain't no shame in their demon worship. I thought you knew but thank God for Jesus Christ. In Mark 16:15-16 Jesus wants us to "Go ye (not sit) into the world, and preach the gospel to every creature. He said, "He that believeth and is baptized shall be saved; but he that believeth not shall be damned." Mark 16:17-18 reminds us "And these signs shall follow them that believe; In my name they shall cast out devils; they shall speak with new tongues; they shall take up serpents; and if they drink any deadly thing, it shall not hurt them; they shall lay hands on the sick, and they shall recover." Thou are holy O thou that inhabited the praises of his people.

Now we can go straight into the presence of God into the Holy of Holies for ourselves without the priest to represent us. Everyone is eligible to have a personal relationship with God. When we get saved we can have an up close and personal relationship with our creator. When we are washed with pure water and the blood of Jesus makes us clean in God's sight.

Remember that temptation is the pull of man's own evil thoughts and wishes. (James 1:14LB), "We must do more than listen to what God is telling us but we must also obey". (James 1:14 KJV), "But every man is tempted, when he is drawn away of his own lust, and enticed." This starts the process of sin in our lives ending in verse15. We must watch what we do. We must act in reverent fear of God now on our way to heaven. We must put on the character of where we are expecting to go. Be holy for God is holy.

Jesus Christ was baptized and received the Holy Spirit and we must do the same and that will give us eternal life. God chose Jesus for this purpose before the world began. Jesus death, burial and resurrection was revealed to us that we will rise again also from the dead. Jesus came and corrected the sin of Adam in the Garden to put us back in right standing with God. Jesus defeated death and when we are saved and obedient we can have life eternal as it was meant to be when man was created. When we are born again not of a woman but of the Spirit gives us life everlasting. Some of the pleasures that we choose to partake of, fight against our soul.

Men are running around this country and don't want any education and don't know how to do anything but destroy their neighborhoods selling drugs in gangs. Every young man or woman wants to run from the police hoping they can make their parents rich if they are shot dead. One soul is worth all the silver and gold on earth. What makes a girl or boy wants to donate themselves to be a slave and become locked up like a beast. When you go to the prison it is like going to the zoo feeding the animals through the fence instead you go to the jail and feed them zoom-zoom and wam-wams through the bars.

These days it takes three or four boys to make a man. They call it a gang. They fight and kill for the earth that God made and they don't even own none of the ground they fight for and kill on. They are the young left alone by their parents feeling unloved. If it was their ground or turf we would hope they would at least pick up the paper and keep it clean.

They only have anger towards themselves to self-destruct. What in hell wrong with you? Men and women are advertising the nastiest part of their bodies. Our mouth is the second nastiest part of our body because of all the dead animals that we put in our mouths to eat. Filthy communication will also bring a world of iniquity.

Women were made from man, for man, by God to nurture the family but many have abandoned their post. A lot of them put on their Jezebel uniform with pony tails and weaves and nails to get naked on the internet for money as they turn their backs on God with open rebellion. They become like wild beast with anybody male, female or animal that has money. They want to meet you. I was wandering who was watching the kids but who is monitoring the adults.

Men are coveting by robbing people of their cars, cell phones, money, and houses of another. They are throwing away their lives with long jail sentences after getting caught and placed into the new slavery by the bad choices that they have made. Women are wearing the Medusa look with long braids that look like snakes that Medusa was curse by Poseidon in a homosexual love affair some kind a way had children. Athena curse Medusa after finding out and took away her beauty. Some women today can't stand to look at themselves or the inner man of the heart with the mirror of the word. Like Medusa they run from the mirror of the word of God with their long nails, wigs, long eye lashes today called their Jezebel rebellious looking uniforms.

Women are leaving their kids to teach themselves at home on the dangerous internet while they pursue man's duty as provider. Isaiah 3:12 says "As for my people, children are their oppressors, and women rule over them. O my people, they which lead thee cause thee to err, and destroy the way of thy paths." God still have his hand stretched out pleading like Noah for them to repent of their sins and come to him before it is too late.

Women are killing babies throwing them in ovens, trash cans like throw away trash. They are aborting babies by the millions. In the first 10 days of January 2021 women and Planned Parenthood killed over 1million babies living in the womb. In June24th 2022 the Supreme Court overturned Roe Vs. Wade saving the lives of millions of babies to prevent Mentally Kidnapped women from murdering more babies.

What in hell wrong with you? Where are all these babies coming from? You say you want a career but you still like to be bare foot and pregnant. This sounds like confusion. Satan is the author of confusion. You can't keep your thighs high to the sky and expect not to get pregnant. You were made for man from man to be fruitful and multiply. Abortion and homosexuality is open rebellion against God not man or the government.

It only offers a first class ticket to hell fire burning. As you can see with open rebellion against God brings flowers on graves and memorials all over the United States of America. Abortion is a sneaky way of saying the child never happened but when you put yourself in the aborted babies place you should not have happened. You were once a fetus and I wonder what would the world be like without you but you are still my horse if you don't ever win a race.

Isaiah 11:1-2, "And there shall come forth a rod out of the stem of Jesse, and a branch shall grow out of his roots: (Vs. 2), "And the spirit of the Lord shall rest upon him, the spirit of wisdom and understanding, the spirit of counsel and might, the spirit of knowledge and of the fear of the Lord." Jesus Christ came so that we may have life but disobedience brings everlasting destruction from the presence of the Lord. Just think burning in the Lake of fire with no hope of being in God's presence who is the only one who can save you. Sin is separation from God.

We must keep our conscience clear so that we can teach the word of God to those whose mind is in a spiritual dungeon and their mind chained down in life. They have to be nurtured as new born babies until they are able to resist sin and sin will begin to lose its power over them. Stay close to them until they can recognize anything that wants to take the place of God in their hearts. Jesus Christ is our message and messenger of life through God's word. This earth is full of the knowledge of the Lord, but the world is rejecting the guidance of the Holy Spirit.

The Holy Spirit is our helper who leads and guides us in the Spirit realm. We are not fighting against flesh and blood but against spiritual wickedness in high places like the Whitehouse. They are opposing and exalting themselves above all that is called God. Satan still wants to be God. The mystery of iniquity is now at work. The only way to get rid of darkness is to love one another by letting the light of Christ shine in us.

When we love the things of the world we become enemies of God. Stay away from greedy people for they are idol worshippers and they love to worship the good things in life more than God who made them. They are like the grave who never have enough. Isaiah 14:9 reminds us that, "Hell from beneath is moved for thee to meet thee at thy coming: it stirreth up the dead for thee, even all the chief ones of the earth; it hath raised up their thrones all the kings of the nations."

Prayer: Ephesians 3:14-21

Heavenly Father I come boldly to your throne in the mighty name of Jesus Christ asking you to reveal and to give me the knowledge opening my understanding in the mystery of Christ. For this cause I bow my knees unto the Father of our Lord Jesus Christ. Of whom the whole family in heaven and earth is named, That he would grant you, according to the riches of his glory, to be strengthen with might by his spirit in the inner man; That Christ may dwell in your hearts by faith; that ye, being rooted and grounded in love, May be able to comprehend with all saints what is the breath, and length, and depth, and height; And to know the love of Christ, which passeth knowledge, that ye might be filled with all the fullness of God. Now unto him that is able to do exceeding abundantly above all that we can ask or think, according to the power that worketh in us, Unto him be glory in the church by Christ Jesus throughout all ages, world without end. Amen.

CHAPTER 7

JESUS IS THE NAME OF GOD

Do you know who God is? Those who are saved will be children of the resurrection because Jesus Christ is the promise of life. 2 Timothy 1:9 says, "Who hath saved us, and called us with a holy calling, not according to our works, but according to his own purpose and grace, which was given us in Christ Jesus before the world began." 1 Timothy 2:5 says, "For there is one God, and one mediator between God and men, the man Christ Jesus." You see, God was not created, born and has no mother or father.

Hebrews 7:3 tells us, "Without father, without mother, without descent, having neither beginning of days, nor end of life; but made like unto the Son of God; abideth a priest continually." Hebrew 7:3LB, Melchizedek's name means "Justice," so he is the King of Justice; and he is also the King of Peace because of the name of his city, Salem, which means "Peace." Melchizedek had no father or mother and there is no record of any of his ancestors. "He was never born and he never died but his life is like that of the Son of God—a priest forever."

He is eternal always never ending and everlasting. God is divine. God has no beginning or end. Jesus the anointed one lived before the spirit got in Mary Joseph exposed. Luke 3:38 says, "Which was the son of E-nos, which was the son of Seth, which was the son of Adam which was first called the son of God." Adams father was God and Jesus father was God. Jesus was the Christ, the Son of God and when you believe ye might have life through his name.

John 17:3, "And this is life eternal, that they might know thee the only true God and Jesus Christ, whom thou sent." Jesus prayed to God when he said the hour has come. In chapter 17:26 he told God I have declared unto them thy name, and will declare it: that the love wherewith thou hast loved me may be in them, and I in them." In 17:6 Jesus said "I have manifested thy name unto the men which thou gavest me out of the world." In 17:11 he said to God, "And now I am no more in the world, but these are in the world, and I come to thee. "Holy Father, keep to thine own name those whom thou hast given me, that they may be one as we are one." Philippians 2:9-10 states that, "Wherefore God hath highly exalted him, and given him a name which is above every name: (Vs.10), "That at the name of Jesus every knee should bow, of things in heaven, and things in earth, and things under the earth."

God is spirit and Jesus is God in Hebrews1:8 reveals, "But unto the Son he saith, Thy throne, O God, is forever and ever; a scepter of righteousness is the scepter of thy kingdom." God is spirit and is a God of his word. God said, "Let us make man in our own image." He was talking with himself and expressing himself who is the Father, and the Holy Ghost. God is Spirit. He said in his word there is no god with me and no god beside me. He was speaking to himself. 1Timothy 3:16, "And without controversy great is the mystery of godliness: God was manifest in the flesh, justified in the Spirit, seen of angels, preached unto the Gentiles, believed on in the world, received up in glory."

God spoke words out of his own will. Isaiah 40:13-14 says, "Who has directed the spirit of the Lord, or being his counsellor has taught him? (Vs.14) "With whom took he counsel, and who instructed him, and taught him in the path of judgement, and taught him knowledge, and shewed to him the way of understanding?" God manifested himself. God hid himself in Jesus. He is a God that hides himself. Isaiah 45:15 tells us that, "Verily thou art a God that hidest thyself, O God of Israel, the Savior." He took upon himself the form of a servant. Jesus took on

God's name. God is spirit and when that spirit got into the man Jesus he began to do the acts of God.

God cannot be tempted but Jesus the man was tempted. James 1:13, "For God cannot be tempted with evil, nor does he tempt anyone." The man Jesus was tempted but the spirit of God cannot be tempted. Mathew 4:1 says, "Then was Jesus led up of the Spirit into the wilderness to be tempted of the devil." Everything that Jesus Christ did was to comply with his God ordained destiny. Christ was manifested in the body or the flesh of Jesus.

Jesus was of the seed of David made earthy but the Spirit of God manifested in the flesh making it holy giving it the power of God. God used that body all the way to the cross. Even after the three days he got back into that body that had no blood and water and the spirit came back in and made the body animated as he walk thru walls as celestial. He came back in a spiritual celestial body that cannot die. He came back into a body that had died in the tomb after taking the keys of death and hell from Satan.

This is the example he came into the world to reconcile us back to himself so that we could be his. This is the process that we will go thru after death. He was sown a natural body and was raised a spiritual. We knew Christ after the flesh but after the resurrection we know him no more. John said He came back in Rev 19:12-13 that, "His eyes were as a flame of fire, and on his head were many crowns, and he had a name written that know man knew, but himself. (Vs.13), "And he was clothed with a vesture dipped in blood: and his name is called the Word of God. Isaiah 51 We must look unto the Rock and that Rock is Jesus. We will be like Jesus when he returns and we will be spiritual or celestial and when we are raised in 1 Corinthians 15:40. "There are also celestial bodies, and bodies terrestrial, but the glory of the celestial is one, and the glory of the terrestrial is another."

Remember the life of the flesh is the blood and flesh and blood cannot inherit the kingdom of God. At the cross blood and water came out and the spirit left at his death when he said "It is Finished." The spirit was three days preaching to all the spirits who had died and was in prison beginning with Adam. The spirit preached to all those who had not heard The Message. The man Jesus from David's seed was tempted but the Holy Spirit that was in him cannot be tempted.

God cannot be tempted. James 1:13-15"Let no man say when he is tempted, I am tempted of God: for God cannot be tempted with evil, neither tempteth he any man: This is the process of sin, Continue, (Vs.14), "But every man is tempted, when he is drawn away of his own lust, and enticed, (Vs.15) "Then when lust hath conceived, it bringeth forth sin, and sin, when it is finished, bringeth forth death."

You see God was in Christ Jesus. 2 Corinthians 5:19, "To wit, that God was in Christ reconciling the world unto himself, not imputing their trespasses unto them; and hath committed unto us the word of reconciliation." God prepared a body in Mary and got in that body after Jesus grew in statue and years because God do not grow in statue and years and he do not have a birthday. God is from Everlasting and he always was. In Hebrews 10:20 shows us God's plan for humankind. "By a new and living way, which he has consecrated for us, through the veil, that is to say his flesh." Our spirits are washed with the word we hear from preachers because God's word is spirit and life. The book of Acts clarifies who God is.

When they stoned Stephen in Acts 7:59, "And they stoned Stephen, calling upon God, and saying Lord Jesus, receive my spirit." Jesus is a Great God in Titus 2:13 and a Just God. There are those who think there is a black god or a white god. They are wrong because God is Spirit. There is no white blood or black blood but only red blood. There is one color in blood. Man made all these denominations by misunderstanding who God is. The Holy Bible shows us that Holiness was here before anything else existed. Christ was alive before His spirit came down like a dove on the body of the man Jesus. He had his name that is everlasting. The body Jesus had a beginning but the spirit that got in that body was from everlasting. But you say how, where, and who gave him his name?

Philippians 2:5-11 says, "Let this mind be in you, which was also in Christ Jesus: (Vs.6), Who, being in the form of God, thought it not robbery to be equal with God: (Vs.7), "But made himself of no reputation, and took upon him the form of a servant, and was made in the likeness of men: (Vs.8), "And being found in the fashion as a man, humbled himself, and became obedient unto death, even death of the cross." (Vs.9), "Wherefore God also hath highly exalted him, and given him a name which is above every name: (Vs.10), "That at the name of Jesus every knee should bow, of things in heaven, and things in earth, and things under the earth." (Vs.11), "And that every tongue should confess that Jesus Christ is Lord, to the glory of God the Father." There is a separation between the human and the divine or the Spirit and the body of Jesus Christ.

John 17:3, "And this is life eternal, that they might know thee the only true God, and Jesus Christ, whom thou hast sent." (Vs.4), I have glorified thee on the earth: I have finished the work which thou gavest me to do. (Vs.5), "And now, O Father, glorify thou me with thine own self with the glory which I had with thee before the world was." (Vs.6), "I have manifested thy name unto the men which thou gavest me out of the world: thine they were, and thou gavest them me; and they have kept thy word." The name of God that he manifested on the earth was Jesus. The child Jesus came in God's name. Jesus never took credit for what the spirit did inside him but he always pointed to the Father who is spirit.

It was the same spirit that got in the body of Jesus after his baptism. In (Vs.11), in chapter 17 of the book of John the flesh talks to God revealing whose name is Jesus. He said Holy Father keep through thine own name those whom thou hast given me that they may be one, as we are." (Vs.12), Jesus name was inherited, "While I was with them in the world, I kept them in thy name: those that thou gavest me."

Isaiah 63:16 says, "Doubtless thou art our father, though Abraham be ignorant of us, and Israel acknowledge us not: thou, O Lord, art our father, our redeemer; thy name is from everlasting." In Hebrews 1:4 says, "Being made so much better than the angels, as he hath by inheritance obtained a more excellent name than they." When you say being made; God is not made because Jesus got his name by inheritance. His name was before Mary and Joseph was born and even before the Tribe of Juda.

Christ was with Moses in 1Corinthians 10:4 says, "And did all drink the same spiritual drink: for they drank of that spiritual Rock that followed them: and that rock was Christ. The flesh profited nothing but it is the spirit that quickens. It is that same spirit in the book of Genesis 1:2, that hovered or moved over the face of the waters. The flesh of Jesus was taught. Mary's baby did not come from heaven, but from the tribe of Juda. The spirit that fell on him after he was baptized was from heaven. Like God who breathe the breath of Life into Adam is the same God who made Mary pregnant.

1 Corinthians 15:45 says "And so it is written, The first man Adam was made a living soul; the last Adam was made a quickening spirit. Jesus Christ put on his earth suit to walk this earth and show us how to walk in the spirit in our bodies. When Jesus walked this earth he said the flesh profited nothing and did not give the flesh any credit instead he always pointed to the Father. It is not of myself but the Father who sent me. The Lord from heaven was made in the image of God in the flesh by the works he did. Jesus would say, if you don't believe me believe the works that I do. He came to man made in God's image but by receiving the Holy Spirit having the fullness of God. God wants us to have that same experience in Ephesians 3:19, "And to know the love of Christ, which passeth knowledge, that ye might be filled with all the fullness of God."

Thank God that Christ bought our freedom with his blood. (Colossians 1:15-19LB), "Christ is the exact likeness of the unseen God. He (Jesus) existed before God made anything at all, and, in fact, (Vs. 16), Christ himself is the Creator, who made everything in heaven and earth, the things we can see and the things we can't; the spirit world with its kings and kingdoms, its rulers and authorities; all were made by Christ for his own use and glory. (Vs.17), He was before all else was began and it is his power that holds everything together. (Vs.18), "He is the Head of the body made up of his people—that is, his church—which he began; and he is the leader of all those who arise from the dead, so that he is first in everything;

Continue: (Vs.19), "for God wanted all of himself to be in his Son. "Christ in your hearts is your only hope for glory." This is done by Christ mighty energy at work in us. Jesus Christ was God's secret plan. "For God's secret plan, now at last made known, is Christ himself"

Colossians 2:2 LB). (Vs.3), In Colossians states, "In him, (Christ) lie hidden all the mighty, untapped treasures of wisdom and knowledge." Colossians 2:9-10 "For in Christ there is all of God in a human body; (Vs.10),so you have everything when you have Christ, and you are filled with God through your union with Christ. He is the highest ruler, with authority over every other power."

Christ was here before Jesus was born in the flesh. He was from eternity and returned to eternity but Mary's baby was from the tribe of Judah but the spirit that fell like a dove after his baptism was from God who is everlasting. 1 Peter 1:20 says, "Who verily was foreordained before the foundation of the world, but was manifested in these last times for you." Jesus was foreordained for sin to come in the world, and he was foreordained to take sin out of the world. John 17:24, "Father, I will that they also, whom thou hast given me, be with me where I am; that they may behold my glory, which thou hast given me: for thou lovest me before the foundation of the world." Titus 1:2 "In hope of eternal life, which God, that cannot lie, promised before the world began." Jesus Christ who is our Shepherd and the Bishop of our souls suffered for us leaving us an example that we should follow his steps.

Jesus Christ is our Creator who made us by his word. 1Peter 4:19 reminds us, "Wherefore let them that suffer according to the will of God commit the keeping of their souls to him in well-doing, as unto a faithful Creator." Godliness makes us fruitful in the knowledge of our Lord Jesus Christ and keeps us established in the present truth. We must know that shortly we will die and our body will unwrap itself from the spirit and we will know the power and coming of our Lord Jesus Christ.

So don't worry, fret, or have anxiety about those spots and blemishes called ministers who will come in their pernicious ways. They will come through covetousness making merchandise of you with feigned words but God know how to deliver you and punish the ungodly in the day of judgement. Your victory is assured by the shed blood of Jesus Christ and praise is the language of faith, "because greater is he that is in you, than he that is in the world." Remember that your victory is assured by the word, the shed blood and the name of Jesus Christ.

He was manifested to take away our sins and he that commits sin is of the devil but the Son of God was manifested to destroy the works of the devil. All unrighteousness is sin. The difference between the holy and the profane is when we get saved and become children of God and those who are not saved are the children of the devil. We should not love God in tongue, nor just words, but in deeds and truth. When we believe on the name of his Son Jesus Christ and abide in him as he abide in us then we will know that he abideth in us by the spirit that he has given us.

We know that every spirit that believes that Jesus Christ is come in the flesh is of God and those who believe not are not of God. They are antichrist and they have the spirit of error. Jesus Christ was sent so that we could live through him by his spirit being in us. When we are born of God by receiving his spirit it makes us world overcomers because we believe that Jesus is the Son of God. We are born of God. Now we should make a record in our minds and heart that God hath given eternal life to those who believe on the name of the Son of God. Jesus Christ got in an earth suit and gave us an understanding that we may know him and be in him that is true and that he is the true God, and eternal life.

Prayer: Colossians 1:9-11

For this cause we also since the day we heard it do not cease to pray for you, and to desire that ye might be filled with the knowledge of his will in all wisdom and spiritual understanding; That ye might walk worthy of the Lord unto all pleasing, being fruitful in every good work, and increasing in the knowledge of God; Strengthen with all might, according to his glorious power, unto all patience, and longsuffering with joyfulness.

CHAPTER 8

IDOLATRY

I would like to remind you that the Lord saved Israel out of Egypt and afterwards destroyed them that believe not. They were those who were groomed to believe and worshipped statues, idols and images. After God delivered Israel out of Egypt, fed them with Manna, gave them water out of a rock and many other great things that he did and they still believed in the golden calf. They still worshiped physical objects as gods. They had immoderate attachment to everything that could not save them.

Idolatry is worshipping anything or person in place of God. Anything that you love, treasure or identify, prioritize or look to for need and fulfilment outside of God can be acting as a god in your life. Then they murmured and complained. They suffered the vengeance of God's eternal fire. They spoke evil about things they knew not without fear. They are mockers that walk after their own ungodly lust. There are idols of men. They are man centered, not God centered. These mockers are imitators, counterfeiters, simulators false prophets that we read about all over the bible. They are leaders that mimic, copy and imitate, acting as and having resembling characteristics of God's chosen ones.

We are living through the mystery of iniquity where the wicked shall be revealed in 2 Thessalonians 2:9. They are those who are doing the workings of Satan with all powers, signs and lying wonders. Today they call themselves miracle workers. God will send strong delusions to those who believe not the truth but will believe a lie. These miracle workers of today are like when God sent Moses and Aaron in Exodus 7:8-12. When Aaron cast down his rod it became a snake. We must remember that there are two miracle workers. God work miracles and so does the devil. Pharaoh also called his wicked sorcerers, and wise men and magicians of Egypt who were not of God and they did some of the same wonders. They did a lying wonder but Aaron's snake swallowed up all their snakes.

So we can't be impressed when we see miracles with signs and wonders. There are people that cast out demons making the lame walk, the blind see and still do not obey God and will not hear from God. God will tell them, depart from me. There was also Simon the sorcerer who acted as though he was some great one in the book of Acts 8:9 who amazed the people of Samaria. Ezekiel 18:20 says the soul that sinneth it shall die. When Moses was on the mount Arron groomed the Israelites to worship the calf. The righteousness of the righteous shall be upon him and the wickedness of the wicked shall be upon him. Satan wants you to die in your sins un-repented of. I don't want your blood on my hands. Once saved always saved is a lie from the pits of hell. You need to read Ezekiel 3:17-21 & Ezekiel 18:20-32 & Ezekiel 33 read all of the chapter.

God gave us a choice to choose all day long. Deuteronomy 30:19, "I call heaven and earth to record this day against you, that I have set before you, life and death, blessing and curses: therefore choose life, that both thou and thy seed may live." We must choose this day who we will serve. Romans 6:16 says whoever you offer yourselves to obey that is your master. "Know ye not, that to whom ye yield yourselves servants to obey, his servants ye are to whom ye obey, whether of sin unto death, or of obedience unto righteousness."

1 John 1:9 says, "If we confess our sins he is faithful and just to forgive us of our sins. The first thing Jesus wants us to do is to repent and that means to turn from our sins. If you think you can get saved and live any way you want too is a lie. You choose your master all day long. God forgave us of our sin past, present and future but shall we

continue in our sin because we are not under the law but under grace. God forbid. "Know ye not that to whom ye yield yourselves servant to obey, his servant ye are to whom ye obey." Romans 6:16

In Ezekiel 33:15 says "If the wicked restore the pledge (Repents of sins) give again that he had robbed, walk in the statues of life, without committing iniquity; he shall surely live." His sins that he committed after he repented are forgiven. If a righteous man turn from his righteousness and committed iniquity and die in his sins all his righteousness shall not deliver him from hell fire burning.

We should ask ourselves by what power was it done? In Exodus 7:19 -21, Moses and Aaron took their rod and stretch forth their hand upon the waters, streams, ponds and rivers and it turned to blood, but the workers of iniquity did the same thing. The magicians of Egypt and those who use enchantments today do lying wonders with no fear of God.

The anti- Christ will be doing miracles through the activity of Satan who attended with great power all kinds of counterfeit miracles in 2Thessalonians 2:9-10. It says, Even him, whose coming is after the working of Satan with all power and signs and lying wonders, (Vs.10), "And with all deceivableness of unrighteousness in them that perish, because they received not the love of the truth, that they might be saved." The people in authority, some millionaires and actors, soothsayers and magicians all workers of iniquity will have to face God at death. God wants obedience and he will tell these miracle workers plainly, I never knew you, depart from me all you workers of iniquity in Mathew 7:23. God's will is for us to hear and obey him.

Anything that you put before god is Idolatry. It is Idolatry when you worship the good things in life before God. Lust of the flesh and the pride of life come from wealth that seems important giving you an exaggerated opinion of your own importance. God allows Satan to attack you and Satan attacks what you are most feared and afraid of losing. You don't have to look for trouble because trouble will find you. Man is born unto troubles. We must seek God first and commit our way unto him. God is a first God.

Like Job said in Job 3:25 "For the thing which I greatly feared is come upon me, and that which I was afraid of is come unto me. Greed is when you want everything that looks good to you and must be obtained at any cost. This will lure you back into sin. Happy is the man whom God corrects. Sin bait looks good in the beginning. Like fish love worms and only get caught by the bait on the hook or in the trap. A trap is not snap shut unless it is first stepped on or in. Once you grab the bait it will be too late. You are caught in sin drawn away by your own lust.

The world is full of greed. The remedy for greed is self-denial. Some of our last hour is fast approaching and those opposing Christ are appearing. Mockers are rebelling openly against God. "Therefore despise not the chastening of the Almighty" Proverb 3:11. The secret of God's wisdom is higher than the heavens and deeper than hell, longer than the earth and broader than the sea. There are those who were with Christ and have left. When they left it shows that they were never with Christ from the beginning. The biggest lie that was ever told was that Jesus Christ is not God's Son. To have the Father you must have his Son who promised us eternal life.

Thank God for the Holy Spirit to help us against sin. God wants us filled with the Holy Spirit's power so that we can fearlessly announce His punishment to the world for their sins. There are people that follow the Lord and worship their Idols in their closets too. They follow the Lord and when time gets tough they get impatient and run to their other gods and idols called casinos, prostitution and drug sales. They go back to their evil customs and pigpens and rob and steal for evil gain from violence and fraud. When Covid 19 came on the scene showed them how powerless their money was when they could not buy another day for those who lost their lives on dying beds. This was a preview when no man will be able to buy or sell without the mark.

There are many who will not face the Lord because their deeds won't permit them to come into his presence. The spirit of idolatry is deep within them. Parents today have shown their children too much deceit. Generational curses is the posterity coming from mothers who are single parents bringing about the curse. In the book of Genesis 27:13

Rebekah told her son Jacob, "And his mother said unto him, "Upon me be the curse, my son only obey my voice, and go and fetch me them."

Rebekah schooled Jacob on how to deceive Isaac his father and told him not to worry about the lie. Kids feel as though their life of crime is acceptable in today's society by the approval of their parents. People are having sex with each other and hating it. This brings about abortion. Men and women did not know that when they had sex with each other that their soul was cleaving to one another when they were having sex becoming one with each other.

When you fornicate you are having sex with every past partner of that person you were then having sex with. All the filthy demons from past sexual relationship were in that bed. We call it experience because we learn from experience with whomever. I say this because people are marrying for the wrong reason. Let's look in the book of Genesis 29th chapter when Jacob married Leah but wanted Racheal. Jacob was having sex with Leah and he was hating it because he loved Rachel. Jacob had married Leah not because he wanted to but for convenience. In verse 31,33, "And when the Lord saw that Leah was hated, he open here womb: but Rachel was barren". Jacob was shooting sperm all over the place by having sex with Rachel and Leah's hand maids.

Some people think school is for fools, but it is quite the opposite. Parents picking favorites should watch themselves. Rebekah told Isaac "Upon me be thy curse", Single parents say that their son can sell drugs and daughter you can sell your body: only obey my voice. "Do not prostitute thy daughter, to cause her to be a whore; lest the land fall to whoredom, and the land become full of wickedness Leviticus 19:29. This is why memorials are being held on every other corner for the deaths that this advice gives. It comes from covetousness wanting that of another. Evil is anything that God is against.

So now it is easy to see who belongs to the Lord and who belongs to Satan. God is truth and love. When we love one another it keeps our conscience clear. There will always be false prophets that will only be around to make their hand happy. Jesus is our only Savior and our only hope from God's terrible anger against sin. Don't be afraid of their faces and don't be afraid of those who preach with false motives or evil purposes in mind but be perfectly straight forward and sincere with them.

The wicked do what the wicked do and those who are Christ do the same as Jesus Christ has written in his Word. You are not inferior unto the wicked because of their status. We will all go down to the grave. How does the rich man die? He dies the same as the fool because we all go down to the grave. We are all fix to the goal of our chosen track at death. At death you will either die in the Lord or out of the Lord.

The Holy Bible says in Revelation 14:13, "And I heard a voice from heaven saying unto me, Write, Blessed are the dead which die in the Lord from henceforth: Yea, saith the Spirit, that they may rest from their labors; and their works do follow them." Don't worry about the forgers of lies and the physicians of no value but keep your mind set on the great physician Jesus Christ and his word for your deliverance.

Hold on to your peace and it will be your wisdom. The nerve of those who will "speak wickedly for God," and "talk deceitfully for him. "God did not ordain homosexual marriage along with many other lies that are being told in the pulpit. There are those who go along just to get along. Who's on the Lord's side come over here? God will do the reproving to those who mock him secretly excepting these persons of sin and abominations.

The left have a lot of money and they are closing the mouth of many preachers. They preach for ratings. It only shows that they have no fear of God and his excellency. They tell God's men to hold their peace, and let them alone and let come upon them what will. Those who turn on God are putting their life in their own hand but believers in Christ are saying "Though he slay me, yet will I trust in him: but I will maintain mine own ways before him"Job13:15. (Vs.1), Job said "who is he that will plead with me? for now, if I hold my tongue, I shall give up the ghost." If you don't speak up now Satan is going to take you all the way out the box with him. Speak now or forever hold your peace.

If a man or woman dies, will they live again? This should be the question we ask ourselves when making daily choices. Woe is me if my soul be wrong five minutes after I die. Humankind should realize that they were not the first man or woman born and God's standard is already set for his creation. The standard is he made woman from man for man. Women should realize what they was made from they was made for. What do they know, that we know not, and what understanding they have that we understand not? God has become small to them.

This is how those who follow Satan think in Isaiah 14:12-14, "How art thou fallen from heaven, O Lucifer, son of the morning! How art thou cut down to the ground, which didst weaken the nations! (Vs.13), "For thou hast said in thine heart, I will ascend into heaven, I will exalt my throne above the stars of God: I will sit also upon the mount of the congregation, in the sides of the north: (Vs.14), "I will ascend above the heights of the clouds; I will be like the most High."

Satan is doing all he can to be a god to Jehovah's creation. The enemy will carry their hearts away from God and turn their spirits against God. Who is man to rebuke God? Humankind is more abominable and drinketh iniquity as water. Those who bald their fist up against God lives will be shorten. They are strengthening themselves against the almighty. We must stand firm in the spirit of God because our conversation and our witness is in heaven. Our record of the way humankind should live is on high.

Those who follow Satan act like they are going to live forever on earth. There spirits will live forever in heaven or hell. I would like to remind them that in just a few years they shall go the way of no return. A few years is enough grace time to change a lot of minds to "Repent" and change what they believe. Don't worship statues, idols and images that can neither hear, nor see. Instead they need spray washing to keep the bird poop off them. Remember that God's word out weigh man who weigh less than air against Jehovah.

Find a bible believing Holy Church that obey the word of God, be baptized in the name of Jesus Christ and receive the gift of the Holy Spirit. Repent and start your walk with God because you got some learning and some growing to do. Eventually you will get it right. God said be ye Holy for I am holy. You are going to need God's Holy Spirit to get into God's kingdom. Those who practice sin will have Satan's spirit to qualify for hell fire burning. Those who love to curse God will forever be in hell fire burning constantly falling into darkness. They will be in hell cursing God because of the wrong choices they made after all the grace time God gave them to come to him. They wonder why they are still alive. It is another opportunity and another day to get it right with God. "Repent" and turn from the sin of Pride.

CHAPTER 9

WE ALL HAVE BOUNDARIES

God has set boundaries that we cannot go beyond. Even the sea has a boundary as big as it is but those that are past shame are past grace and now past hope. The alphabet group or the Left are past shame. Those who mislead us cause us to err using their power wrong by mentally kidnapping the minds of God's creation into willful sin. Leaders that pass gun laws are terrorizing our society by making it lawless. They are chipping away the protection of our government by trying to take away our earthly angels, the police.

These men have weak judgment and strong passions as women and children are ruling our nation. God has already set the standard. Woe is coming to the wicked as the righteous keep themselves pure. I don't know what Woe is but I sure don't want none of it. The daughters of Zion will be indicted for haughtiness and wantonness by their inherent qualities of their mind and character and turn of mind. Their disposition and layout is not lining up with the word of God in the action of distributing or transferring property and money as a power lever.

So now children become their oppressors. God said in Isaiah 3:11-13), "Woe to the wicked! It shall be ill with him: for the reward of his hands shall be given him." "As for my people, children are their oppressors, and women rule over them. O my people, they which lead thee cause thee to err, and destroy the way of thy paths." "The Lord standeth up to plead, and standeth to judge the people." Isaiah 9:16 says, "For the leaders of this people cause them to err; and they that are led of them are destroyed." (Vs.17), "Therefore the Lord shall have no joy in their young men, neither shall have mercy on their fatherless and widows: for every one is a hypocrite and an evil doer, and every mouth speaketh folly. "For all this his anger is not turned away, but his hand is stretched out still."

Humankind has boundaries. Job 14:5 states that, " Seeing his days are determined, the number of his months are with thee, thou hast appointed his bounds he cannot pass. This speaks of life here on earth. "And set a bolt and doors, and I said, Thus far you shall come, but no further…"For I have placed the sand as a boundary for the sea." Proverbs 8:29 says "When he set a boundary for the sea, so that the waters would not surpass His command when He marked out the foundations of the earth. Job 14:16-17 remind us, "For now thou numberest my steps: dost thou not watch over my sin? (Vs.17), "My transgression is sealed up in a bag, and thou sawest mine iniquity."

This is God's wisdom talking. In Jeremiah 5:22 says "For I have placed the sand as a boundary for the sea. "An eternal decree and a perpetual barrier beyond which it cannot pass it, and though the waves thereof toss themselves, yet can they not prevail; though they roar, yet can they not pass." God marked the foundations of the earth. Before he made the earth or its field or any of the dust of the earth when he gave the sea its boundary so the waters would not over step his command, and when he marked out the foundations of the earth rejoicing in his whole world and delighting in mankind.

Our government seems to want a one world government, a welfare state of government that is being run by the Left who defy Jehovah our creator. Men loving men, and women loving women is their bedside manner. Regardless it is still offensive to God. The Left can only go as far as God let them. God said, in Job 38:29, "Out of whose womb came the ice? and the hoary frost of heaven, who has gendered it?" God has already decreed gender so why keep playing with your own mind? Fighting against Jehovah is a figment of your imagination.

In God's eyesight gay marriage do not exist. They may be proud but even the evil and wicked spirit inside them cannot instruct God. God said in Job 38:9-11, "When I made the cloud the garment thereof, and thick darkness a swaddling band for it," (Vs. 10), "And break up for it my decreed place, and set bars and doors," (Vs.11)"And said, Hitherto shalt come, but no further: and here shall thy proud waves be stayed?" When your sin cup is full then God brings his judgement.

The media promotes these evils as they project the lies of the devil into our homes. Programing its citizens minds to accept this new world that is a figment of their imagination. They want to transfer the thoughts in their minds so you will live in their world. Our world wants to go off the cliff. They want to self- destruct. The left is working 24-7 and are not sleeping to take the world down the drain. They are agents of Satan and only come to steal, kill and to destroy. Satan' emissaries show the leaders of our country that are taking our country at a fast pace that it can't stop and rethink itself to make a better decision about its future.

What I am saying is the Left is taking our country at a fast past to prove a point that people can do anything they want. Especially the alphabet group and women can do the job of a man and it will only be to their own hurt. When they hurt family they hurt the world. God has set boundaries that none of us can pass even the scientist cannot pass God's boundaries. When George Floyd died at the hand of terrorist police, the officer's trial started an awakening that there are boundaries that we cannot cross.

When we speak God's word it makes us a messenger of his truth and don't change it one bit to suit the taste of those who hear it. We serve God alone and he examines our hearts deepest thoughts. False prophets are against God and man. Getting sinners saved should be our hope and joy. When I got saved I felt as though I had just won first place. I was holding my trophy and wearing my crown of salvation.

Revelation 3:11 KJV says, "Behold, I come quickly: hold that fast which thou hast, that no man take thy crown". James 1:12 KJV "Blessed is the man that endureth temptation: for when he is tried, he shall receive the crown of life, which the Lord hath promised to them that love him. "And when the chief Shepherd shall appear, ye shall receive a crown of glory that faded not away."

So count this as joy when someone receives Jesus Christ as Lord and Savior from you doing the Gospel's work and that will be your trophy when you stand before Christ. God the Father has made us strong, sinless and holy on that day when Jesus returns with those who love him. So remain strong in him. Stay close and plugged into the Lord who is your source of power.

2 Thessalonians 1:7-8 Living Bible says, "And so I would say to you who are suffering, God will give you rest along with us when the Lord Jesus appears suddenly from heaven in flaming fire with his mighty angels, bringing judgement on those who do not wish to know God, and who refuse to accept his plan to save them through our Lord Jesus Christ." But don't get upset or excited because of false prophets spreading rumors or having special messages from God about this. Don't be carried away and deceived regardless of what they say.

Satan is using people as tools that work effectively on those who say no to the Truth and have refused to believe and love the Truth so that it could save them. So God let them believe lies and falsehood with all their heart as they enjoy their sins. Even though God called them to enjoy and share in the glory of Jesus Christ. The Lord is faithful and will save you from satanic attacks from evil men and women.

Remember that the God of peace of untroubled, undisturbed wellbeing will be with you. 1 John 2:18 says, "Little children, it is the last hour; and as you have heard that the Antichrist is coming, even now many antichrist have come, by which we know that it is the last hour." Let the peace of Christ rule in your hearts" Colossians 3:15. "Thou will keep him in perfect peace whose mind is stayed on thee because he trusteth in thee" Isaiah 26:3.

Take authority over your thought life. We live in the flesh but we are not carrying on our warfare according to the flesh using mere human weapons. 11Corinthians 10:4 says, "For the weapons of our warfare are not carnal, but mighty through God to the pulling down of strongholds." We must refute or prove a statement or theory to be wrong or false. To disprove arguments and theories and reasoning and every proud and lofty thing that set itself up against the (true) knowledge of God.

Bring those thoughts into the obedience of Christ, the Messiah, the Anointed One. Keep your mind in the presence of God and glorify God with your spirit, soul and body. Forgive and let go past wrongs and move fast forward with your mind set on things above the higher things, not the things on the earth.

When we look at the patience of God it will give us a deeper understanding of his giving us what we don't deserve; his grace. Don't forget that Truth is the Supreme authority superior to all others, the Supreme reality, the ultimate meaning and value of existence which is the state of living independent of the mind. It is not a place to defend your preferred point of view. 1 John 4:4 NLB, "But you belong to God, my dear children. You have already won a victory over those people, because the Spirit who lives in you is greater than the spirit who lives in the world."

God sent his Son into the world to show his love to us to give us eternal life. If you can say and believe that Jesus is the Son of God then God is living on the inside of you. Being a Child of God you have to stay plugged in so that his love can bless you. Don't unplug yourself from the source of God's power.

Stay off the road of the wicked. Instead stay on God's Holy Highway for his peace, joy, love and protection. We are living in a time when Satan's merchandise is being sold by his merchants in the earth but you stick with the free gifts of God. Stay plugged into your Holy Scriptures so that you will not buy into their goods. Satan wants to sell you water, air and even the ground you walk on but you remember the earth is the Lords and the fullness thereof and all that dwell therein. You got to know the things that are freely given unto you. Remember you are an heir of God and a joint heir with Jesus. You are an heir to the blessing of Abraham (Romans 8:17, Galatians 3:13, 14). You are a child of God and a Son of God Romans 8:16, Romans 8:14.

Luke 12:32 Bible Gateway says, "Do not be seized with alarm and struck with fear, little flock" For it is God's good pleasure to give you the kingdom." God wants to make you rich in every area of your life.

He don't want you to be sick, broke and lonely. "It is the blessing of the Lord that maketh rich and addeth no sorrow with it Proverb 10:22. Remember in Deuteronomy 8:18, " But thou shall remember the Lord thy God: for it is he that giveth thee power to get wealth, that he may establish his covenant." Psalms 23 "The Lord is my shepherd I shall not want."

Continue: Philippians 4:19, "But my God shall supply all your needs according to his riches and glory by Christ Jesus." I do not worry, fret, or have anxiety about anything. I do not have a care Philippians 4:6, 1Peter 5:6-7. God blesses us to be a blessing with health, love, talent= the special favor, mercy or benefit along with the blessing of liberty. Psalms 50:10 tells us he is the God of the cattle upon a thousand hills. "For every beast of the forest is mine, and the cattle upon a thousand hills." We thank him for increase and for having all sufficiency in all things so we may abound in every good work and charitable donation in the mighty name of Jesus Christ we pray, Hallelujah.

Remember to put your faith and trust in Jehovah because money make wings and fly away and in Revelation 18:17 ESV says in one moment all the wealth is gone. "For in a single hour all this wealth has been laid waste." In the Kings James version says, "For in one hour so great riches is come to nought." We had a preview in Covid 19 of how everything can be shut down in an instance. Every one stopped what they were doing and took thought about their soul. Our soul is the most important thing that we possess. The world is becoming dens of demons of devils and every kind of evil spirit.

Our days are numbered. This could be your last chance before your world ends, not the end of the world, but the end of your world. Death could be around the next corner. No man knows the day or the hour when Jesus will return. Psalms 90:12 says, "So teach us to number our days, that we may apply our hearts unto wisdom." After Jesus was tempted in the wilderness came the beginning of the gospel of Jesus Christ, the Son of God." Mark 1:15 says "And saying, The time is fulfilled, and the kingdom of God is at hand: repent ye, and believe the gospel." "All scripture is given by inspiration of God, and is profitable for doctrine, for reproof, for correction, for instruction in righteousness:

"That the man of God may be perfect thoroughly furnished unto all good works" 2 Timothy 3:16-17.

Humble yourself before God and he will lift you up. Get to know him more to understand his great power. God will supply you with all you need when you ask. Asking for something might seem strange to a proud person or Satan who only comes to steal, kill and to destroy. God teaches his children to ask. You have not because you ask not. God knows your need before you ask but he wants you to trust and believe in him. He wants you to know the things that are freely given unto you. God wants you to have his character this is why he made you in his image.

God can keep you from temptations that surround you and still punish the evil ones around you. I am living in a building full of evil and I can witness to that. Psalms 91 says "A thousand may fall by your side and ten thousand by your right hand but it shall not come nigh thee." Some say you might as well do what you want to do because being good don't help you. When you do what you want to do by being your own god will only make you free to self-destruct. That's why Jesus came and that was to keep us from self-destructing. God wants to show you his goodness so you can be a witness for yourself how good he is.

Jesus Christ came to keep us from guilt, shame and condemnation. Why would you want to lie to yourself first of all refusing to accept the truth about your sins? You are afraid to look in the mirror like women looking like the Medusa. Some women of today look like winged human females with living venomous snakes in place of hair. Those who gazed in her eyes would turn to stone. They wear their hair long in braids like snakes. They are rebellious openly and will not look at themselves when they put on their Jezebel uniform. Why would you want to be the first person you lie to? We need to own our sins. 1 John 1;8 says if we say that we have no sin we are lying (Vs.10)," If we claim we have not sinned we are lying and calling God a liar, for he says we have sinned."

Jesus took away our sins upon himself to bring us back into fellowship with Jehovah God our creator. When Adam and Eve dropped the ball by sinning in the Garden of Eden Jesus became the forgiveness for our sins. He became our scapegoat. He died, was buried and rose again and he blessed us by sending us the Holy Spirit to live in us. He tore down the vail or wall between man and God and put us back in right standing with our creator. Now we can go into God's presence as often as we like. In his presence is fullness of joy and pleasures forever more.

God wants to forgive you of your sin and that of the whole world. We must examine ourselves constantly by looking into the mirror of the Word of God. Are you confused about what temple to worship in? You are the temple of God. The Goliath's in our life have a big shield in front of them. So let's take the smooth stone of the word and aim at the brain of our adversary. Let that smooth stone be the Truth about Jesus Christ so that we can run strait to our giants in life with no hesitation.

God is bigger than any problem that we may face and his word produce good things into our lives and into the lives of others. Jehovah our God is the Supreme Authority above all other spirits, powers, and principalities. When we choose God's word for our lips we choose God's will for our life. So be bold as a lion and go forth and perform them in Jesus mighty name we pray.

Jehovah is the Supreme reality; the ultimate meaning and value of existence. He is the Truth that will set you free. "2 Timothy 3:16-17 says, "The whole Bible was given to us by inspiration from God and is useful to teach us what is true and to make us realize what is wrong in our lives; it straightens us out and helps us do what is right. (Vs.17), It is God's way of making us well prepared at every point, fully equipped to do good to everyone." We should submit all to God, Prayers that Avails much Men. "Father, thank You for pastors and leaders of the church—those who are submitted to You and are examples to the congregation. I submit to the church elders the ministers and spiritual guides of the church—giving them due respect and yielding to their counsel." I thank you Lord for being in me, on me, around me and for me.

We must put our faith and belief in God and into the obedience of his word. Hebrew 4:12-13 LB "For whatever God says, to us is full of living power: it is sharper than the sharpest dagger, cutting swift and deep into our innermost thoughts and desires with all their parts, exposing us for what we really are. (Vs.13), He knows about everyone, everywhere. Everything about us is bare and wide open to the all -seeing eyes of our living God, nothing can be hidden from him to whom we must explain all that we have done."

We have to practice doing right. In the seventh chapter in the book of Hebrews says "Yes, the old system of priesthood based on family lines was canceled because it did not work. "Under the old arrangement there had to be many priest, so that when the older ones died off, the system could still be carried on by others who took their place" Hebrews 7:23LB. The next verse tells us that "But Jesus lives forever and continues to be Priest so that no one else is needed." "He is able to save completely all who come to God through him."

Jesus Christ was our sacrifice on the cross who is perfect forever and gave us eternal salvation. If God is spirit then how was Jesus Christ body made ready to lay on the altar of God in heaven? He is spirit because we know that flesh and blood cannot inherent the kingdom of God. We have been forgiven and made clean by Christ dying once and for all. Now that one offering was made forever perfect in the sight of God and it is now making us holy. Our sins have been forever forgiven and forgotten.

Now we don't have to run, duck and hide from God when we sin. We can just run straight into the presence of God repenting of our sin with a sincere heart to take away guilt, cowardness and condemnation. Remember that our faith in him assures our salvation. Without faith it is impossible to please him. What is faith? It is the confident assurance that something we want is going to happen. It is the certainty that what we hope for is waiting for us, even though we cannot see it up ahead" (Hebrews 11:1 LB).

We must learn to know God better and better and he will give us his own character. He wants to give us a good life and share his glory and goodness with us. He wants to make you look good as you represent the Father and Jesus well. We must put aside our own desires to find out what God wants us to do. God want you to grow in love and the fullness and fellowship with others. When you grow in your love walk which is one of the fruit of the spirit you become useful to the Lord. Our love walk with the Lord is not a selfish walk because everything that God gives us is for us to share with others.

Remember there will be false prophets in our midst that will tell clever lies about God. They will turn against the one who paid the price on the cross for them. They will continue scoffing Christ in their teaching that there is nothing wrong with sexual sin. This reminds me of the TV show the Adams family. Homosexuals think their home is normal just like the Adam's family. Monsters in the Adam's family believe that everyone else is abnormal and they are normal. When normal people or people that love God come into the Adam's family house they leave out of there screaming with fear.

The same is when a child of God goes into a house with same-sex marriage. People know they are in a house of insanity when two men or two women act as though they had these children. In their mind they think they are perfectly normal and you can't make them believe otherwise. There are evil spirits that possess them and they have been turned over into a reprobate mind that they should believe a lie. Be encouraged that God condemned them long ago and threw them into hell and caves and darkness in chains. God condemned those that perished who were before the flood all except Noah. God saved Noah because he spoke up for God, and his family of seven. God also reduced Sodom and Gomorrah into ashes and deleted them off the face of the earth.

God did this to remind the Left group that would come in our times to look back and fear. God rescued Lot and his family because God was sick of all the lust and wickedness all around his people infesting their character. God will also rescue us from the temptation that surround us today and will continue to punish the wicked around us. False teachers are fools and are no better than animals born only to be caught and killed.

They mock heaven and hell as they laugh at hell fire burning. They don't realize that they will be destroyed along with all the demons and powers of hell. They continue in evil pleasures daily and sit and eat with God's children deceiving themselves and the church. They make a sport of alluring unstable women with their lust and greed. They are cursed and they spread the curse as a sin virus. They have gone off the road of the Holy Highway and have fell in love with money instead of love for

Jehovah. They are like a glass with no water in it. Their conversation is mostly about themselves and not the Gospel of Christ. They give those who are fresh out of their sins no strength but they lure them back into sin.

They tell them to do as you please and enjoy your life putting hardly any biblical restrictions on them. It is better to have never known Christ and his laws than to know them and to turn your back on them. A dog comes back to what he has vomited, and a pig is wash only to come back and wallow in the mud again. This is what it looks like when a person returns to his sin. In these last days scoffers will do as they please and they will do every wrong they can think of. This is why we must be rooted and grounded in the word of the Living God.

People continue in their sin because Jesus has not returned and they don't believe that he will because they forgot how God already destroyed the world with the flood. He did it not long after he had made the world just by speaking it into existence. They say there has nothing changed since the beginning of creation. When you get saved the change comes through you. Jesus our Lord and Savior is coming back for those living in Christ Jesus and those who have been dead for a long time. It will be in a moment in the twinkling of the eye. So we must be like Johnny Taylor we must be, "Ever Ready."

They forgot that there will be a barn fire for the unjust on judgement day when all sinners will perish in that fire. One day is as a thousand years to God. God is waiting on them to surrender because he wish that all should be saved In the book of 2 Peter 3:12LB says, You should look forward to that day and hurry it along the day when God will set the heavens on fire, and the heavenly bodies will melt and dis- appear in flames." The reason why God is waiting is because, "He is giving us time to get his message of salvation out to others" 2 Peter 3:15 LB. For those who are stupid on purpose who twist God's word to mean something different will result in their own doom. We should thank God for his grace giving us another opportunity to get it right because it does not seem like none of us is really ready.

So I also warn you not to get caught up in the mistakes of the wicked and you become mixed up too. 2 Peter 3:18 LB, "But grow in spiritual strength and become better acquainted with our Lord and Savior Jesus Christ. Give him the glory and honor now and forever more. "But those who keep on sinning are against God, for every sin is done against the will of God." Only God is holy, only God is good. He prescribed righteousness and prescribed rebellion and both righteousness and rebellion find their meaning in God because God is our standard. People keep on sinning because they have never really known him or become his. When we are born again you just cannot keep on sinning because of the conviction of your heart.

When you receive Jesus Christ as Lord over your life God's life is in you. God's new life has been born into him or her so he or she can't keep on sinning. They are born again and the new life in Christ controls him. If you are afraid of God and run from him when you do wrong shows that you are not fully convinced that God really love you. We must love God who has perfect love for us and our brothers and sisters too. If you love the Father then you should love his Son too. Your actions of obedience will show how much you love God. Obeying God with confidence and joy shows your love as you resist and defeat sin and evil pleasure by trusting Christ to help you.

We must believe that Jesus is the Son of God. 1 John 5:6-8, reminds us that, "And we know he is, because God said so with a voice from heaven when Jesus was baptized, and again as he was facing death—yes, not only at his baptism but also as he faced death. "And the Holy Spirit, forever truthful, says it too. So we have these three witnesses: the voice of the Holy Spirit in our hearts, the voice from heaven at Christ baptism, and the voice before he died. "And they all say the same thing: that Jesus Christ is the Son of God." "All who believe this know in their hearts that it is true."

Continue: "If anyone doesn't believe this, he is actually calling God a liar, because he doesn't believe what God said about his Son" (1 John 5:10 LB). (Vs.11), "God hath said? That he has given us eternal life and that this life is in his Son." (Vs.12), "So if you don't have the Son, you do not have life, but if you do, you have life." (18), "No one who has become part of God's family makes a practice of sinning, For Christ, God's Son, holds him securely and the devil cannot get his hands on him." (Vs.19), "We know that we are children of God and that all the rest of the world around us is under Satan's power and control." (Vs.20), "And we know that Christ, God's Son, has come to help us understand and find the true God. And now we are in God because we are in Jesus Christ his Son, who is the only true God; and he is eternal life."

We must always stay in God's boundaries where God's love can reach and bless us. God wants to give you fruit from the Tree of Life in the Paradise of God. We are surrounded by Satan devotees of sin in a nation where Satan's throne is the center of satanic worship. Stay loyal to Jesus Christ and refuse to deny him instead resist the devil and he will flee from you. Our leaders are ruining the people while leading them into sexual sin and encouraging idol worship. There is a great need for God's children to speak with the sword of his word to change their mind and attitude. Those who can hear God's voice must listen to what the Spirit is saying to the churches. Do not fear because God wants to give to you hidden manna the secret nourishment from heaven to assist you.

Don't think that God don't see your good deeds of kindness to the poor. He sees your gifts of kindness, faith, love and patience. God is concerned about that Jezebel Spirit that our country is allowing to practice sex sins. God has given us his grace and that is more time to change and obey his word. His grace is God giving us what we don't deserve. God wants us to repent of our sins especially those who follow the immoral teachings of Jezebel. God searches deep within the mind and hearts of men and women. He is going to give each one of us whatever we deserve. You see our ex sins are all about money and coveting that between another's legs. The world's wisdom calls them "deeper truths" and they are from the depths of Satan.

God wants his followers to stay rooted and grounded in his word until he returns. God wants to give you power to rule and give to you the Morning Star in Revelation 2:26-28 Paraphrase. God wants his church to Wake-Up and Snap out of it. Strengthen what little that you have left. Can't you see that you are almost at the point of death. Go back to, "In the beginning" and hold firmly to it and turn to God. When you first got saved you had the fire of God in you. God wants you to have his image and for you to know who you are in Christ Jesus.

CHAPTER 10

DO YOU KNOW WHO YOU ARE?

Once you realize who you are in Christ Jesus the devil and all the demons in hell can't stop you when you have the power of God's word encouraging, uplifting and motivating you. Remember, God gave you keys for your success in his word to overcome. God gave us Titled: "My Keys to Success". Go back to the beginning when you were on fire for God. Do your I am Affirmations. I know you remember them. They start off like this!

"This book of the Law shall not depart out of (my) mouth; but (I) shall meditate therein day and night, that (I) mayest observe "to do" according to all that is written therein: for then (I) shalt make (my) way prosperous, and then I shall have good success. "Have I not commanded thee to be strong and of a good courage be not afraid neither be thou dismayed for the Lord thou God is with thee withersoever thou goest" (Joshua 1:8-9).

God is interested in your spiritual, emotional, and psychological growth and well- being. Knowing who you are in Christ will help you grow and become the overcomer that God created you to be. Listed here are several scriptural affirmations based on your new life in Christ. Recite these daily until they become a part of your new life and consciousness. Preface each affirmation with "I am." Example: "I am a child of God, I am redeemed from the hand of the enemy." Say this until you have completed all 43 affirmations.

1. I am a child of God (Romans 8:16)
2. I am redeemed from the hand of the enemy (Psalms 107:2)
3. I am forgiven (Colossians 1:13,14)
4. I am saved by grace through faith (Ephesians 2:8)
5. I am Justified (Romans 5:1)
6. I am Sanctified (1 Corinthians 6:11)
7. I am a new creature (2 Corinthians 5:17
8. I am Partaker of His divine nature (2Peter 1-4)
9. I am Redeemed from the curse of the law (Galatians 3:13)
10. I am Delivered from the powers of darkness (Colossians 3:13)
11. I am Led by the Spirit of God (Romans 8:14)
12. I am A Son of God (Romans 8:14)
13. I am Kept in safety wherever I go (Psalms 91:11)
14. I am Getting all my needs met by Jesus (1Peter 5:7)
15. I am Casting all my cares on Jesus (1Peter 5:7)
16. I am Strong in the Lord and in the power of his might (Ephesians 6:10)
17. I am Doing things through Christ who strengthens me (Philippians 4;13)
18. I am an Heir of God and a joint heir with Jesus (Romans 8:17)
19. I am Heir to the blessing of Abraham (Galatians 3:13,14)
20. I am Observing and doing the Lord's commandments (Deut. 28:12)
21. I am Blessed coming in and going out (Deuteronomy 28:6)
22. I am an Inheritor of eternal life (1John 5:11,12)
23. I am Blessed with all spiritual blessing (Ephesians 1:3)
24. I am Healed by His Stripes (1Peter 2:24)
25. I am Exercising my authority over the enemy (Luke 10:19)
26. I am Above only and not beneath (Deut. 28:13)
27. I am More than a conqueror (Romans 8:37)
28. I am Establishing God's Word here on earth (Mathew 16:19)
29. I am an Overcomer by the blood of the Lamb and the word of my testimony (Rev. 12:11)

30. I am Daily overcoming the devil (1John 4:4)
31. I am Not moved by what I see (2Corinthians 5:7)
32. I am Walking by faith and not by sight (2 Cor.5:7)
33. I am Casting down vain imaginations (2 Corinthians 10:4-5)
34. I am Bringing every thought into captivity (2Cor. 10:5)
35. I am Being transformed by a renewed mind (Romans 12:1-2)
36. I am Labored together with God (1 Cor. 3:9)
37. I am The righteousness of God in Christ Jesus (2 Corinthians 5:21)
38. I am An imitator of Jesus (Ephesians 5:1)
39. I am The Light of the world (Mathew 5:14)
40. I am Learning Truth and that Truth makes me free (John 8:32)
41. I am Chosen and ordained to bring forth fruit (John 15:16)
42. I am a Recipient of peace (John14:2
43. I am Confident of a good work being done in me (Philippians 1:6).

Confess Who You Are in Christ! Knowing who you are in Christ will change your life dramatically. As you begin to confess these truths daily, your faith will increase, your life will change for the better. You will have health, prosperity (both spiritually and financially) and the abundant life that Jesus came to provide for you. (John 10:10) Try confessing these 43 truths for 21 consecutive days, and watch how your life will change for the better! Faith comes by hearing and hearing by the word of God. (Romans 10:17) Praise God. Jesus is real!

Always remember these Four Principles on Which to Live Your Life!
God is Who He says He is.
God will do what He says He will do.
You are who God says you are.
You can do what God says you can do.
Choose All Day Long

Each day that we live is a gift; yes life is a gift. It is never too late to be what you want to be. When you say I can do all things through Christ means I can do everything God wants me to do. We need evidence, confidence and confirmation. The worst enemy that you will ever confront is yourself overweight, jobs, and education. Jesus said in Revelation 3:20 "Look I have been standing at the door and I am constantly knocking. If anyone hears me calling him and opens the door, I will come in and fellowship with him and he with me."

The name of God is Jesus. The body of Jesus was not God. God came into the body of Jesus by spirit not the picture on your wall or cross around your neck. Numbers 3:52 says "destroy all their pictures, and destroy all their molten images, and quite pluck down all their high places." Places of worship for those who did not worship the God of Israel were called high places. God is Spirit and those who worship him must worship him in spirit and truth. Jesus received the spirit the way we are to receive him. He came to show us how to walk in that Spirit to have victory over the devil.

Remember Jesus is the word that spoke the generations of heaven and the earth in that day that the Lord God made the heavens and the earth. When the Lord God formed every beast of the field, and fowls of the air, he brought them to Adam to name. "Whatsoever Adam called every living creature, that was the name thereof." Humankind wants to duplicate the Lord God by putting man to sleep and adding to what God has created through surgery. Opening and closing the flesh like God when he performed the first surgery and took the rib of man and made the woman out of man and brought her unto him.

Now Satan is trying to duplicate the Lord God through mad scientist and some surgeons by putting man asleep and opening the flesh of man making him a woman and bringing more abominations into the world. Mad scientist wants to make man pregnant but the only way man can get pregnant is by being born again by the spirit of God. Satan is giving man his own rib by giving man another man. In his own mind he calls himself woman. Now all births come through a woman even test tube babies.

"Therefore shall a man leave his father and mother, and cleave unto his wife, and they shall be one flesh" (Genesis 2:24 KJV). In verse 25 says, "And they were both naked, the man and his wife, and were not ashamed," until the serpent showed up in chapter 3. This is when the lust of the eye and the flesh came to humankind. This is when guilt, shame and condemnation came into the world. Their eyes were opened. Today men and women are beyond shame making them ripe for hell. This is the reason why God exiled humankind from the earth in Noah's days. It was forced removal from the earth. Humankind was banished voluntarily because of their disobedience by bringing on them a self-imposed absence.

Satan is still at work on the woman because "thy desire should be to thy husband and he shall rule over thee". After the sin in the Garden of Eden, God laid out the sentence to Adam, Eve and Satan. Adam continued with his naming. So he called his wife name Eve because she was the mother of all living, not trans-ves-tite. Transvestite is a person who dresses in clothes associated with that of the opposite sex. Transgender is a man or woman assigned by God at birth male or female, but the mind of Satan transforms into trans- man or trans-woman, Satan's merchandise.

Her son Cain and all the Cain's of the earth today are being "curse from the earth which hath opened her mouth to receive thy brother's blood from their hand." Most parents and teachers ask kids what do you want to be when you grow up? Kids would usually respond a doctor, fireman or a teacher. Now they want to be anything that has the merchandise of Satan. A fugitive and a vagabond with pants hanging down in the earth is what they desire dead or in prison. What is so desirable about prison that makes them want to go is beyond me? They want to be anywhere except in the presence of God.

There is still hope because Cain and his wife conceived Enoch who walked with God. OK Jared son of Mahalaleel also begat a son called Enoch after living 162 years, but Jared lived 962 years and died. Enoch son of Jared walked with God. Enoch begat Methuselah. He was the man that lived longer than any other man alive on earth. He lived 969 years.

God set a new standard for humankind because of their evil continually. He set 120 yrs. then three score and ten. That was a lot of candles on Methuselah's cake. Noah walked with God. The earth today is filled with violence and corruption. Mathew 3:7 reminds the leaders of our churches, "But when he saw many of the Pharisees and Sadducees come to his baptism, he said unto them, "O generation of vipers, who hath warned you to flee from the wrath to come."

God gives us a reason to walk closely with him. God even told Noah before he was going to destroy the earth to bring two of every sort of animal into the ark. He wanted to keep them alive with Noah. Animals came on their own two by two. He did not say, bring the alphabet group and transgender because this sin sickness was in the mind not the body. The Lord God told him to bring male and female. Two of every sort shall come unto thee, to keep them alive. God was destroying humankind because of wickedness. He did not destroy the earth but the wickedness in humankind on the earth. The next time the earth's wickedness is destroyed it will be by fire and God will make a new heaven and a new earth.

In Revelation 21:1says, "And I saw a new heaven and a new earth: for the first heaven and the first earth were passed away; and there was no more sea." All the beast and fowls of the air Noah brought male and female. God was about to destroy every living substance. He destroyed all wickedness in man and every imagination of the thoughts of his heart that was evil continually.

God told Noah to bring male and female to the Ark to repopulate, but our government have same sex to depopulate. Since these cursed laws of abortion and same sex marriage were passed our world has been doing every- thing to depopulate the earth. Now Satan use mad Scientist to spread disease (Covid 19) and monkey pox over the world to depopulate the world.

CHAPTER 11

LEARN THESE SCRIPTURES FOR GROWTH, PROSPERITY, AND SUCCESS IN LIFE!

Meditate on the scriptures. "All scriptures is given by inspiration of God, and is profitable for doctrine, for reproof, for correction, for instruction in righteousness: that the man of God may be thoroughly furnished unto all good works" 11 Timothy 3:16-17.

As a born again believer, it is important to your growth and success in life that you feed on the word of God. It will provide strength, life, and life more abundantly for you. For Jesus said when he was tempted by the devil, "Man shall not live by bread alone, but by every word that proceedeth out of the mouth of God" Mathew 4:4).

Just as it is vital for your natural body to eat natural food in order to grow strong, it is just as important that you feast on the word of God in order for your spiritual man inside you to grow strong to defend against the attacks of the enemy.

As new born babies, desire the sincere milk of the word, that ye may grow thereby: If so be ye have tasted that the Lord is gracious." Remember, the word of God is also the sword of the Spirit and a part of your armor and your only offensive weapon against the devil. "And take the helmet of salvation and the sword of the Spirit, which is the word of God" Ephesians 6:17.

CHAPTER 12

DEVELOP A PERSONAL RELATIONSHIP WITH GOD

If you have not already done so, ask Jesus to become your Lord and Savior. In your own words "Repent of your sins and ask God to forgive you of all your sins and to make you a new creature. Now be baptized in the name of Jesus Christ and receive the gift of the Holy Spirit with the evidence of speaking in tongues. We must tarry until we receive the gift of the Holy Spirit. When you have received the Lord and have a personal relationship with Him, it is a joy to talk with Him and learn about Him through His word.

As you read God's word, you can talk with him, and He talks with you. By reading and meditating on the word of God you have communion with him and a fulfilled life, and God's abundance will permeate your entire being. You begin to know Him and His will for your life. All the joy, strength, and knowledge of God become yours as you meditate day and night on His word. Jude 1:1 says Jude, the servant of Jesus Christ, and brother of James, to them that are sanctified by God the Father, and preserved in Jesus Christ, and called."

We have to be sanctified from our self. Roman 7 tells us our own will try to keep us from obeying God. There are two laws where the flesh and spirit war against each other. We must beat the law of the flesh into subjection with the power of the Holy Spirit and the unadulterated, unchanging, uncompromising living word of God. God's word is alive and when we speak it makes it alive and working in us. That will make God alive and working in us. When we choose God's word for our lips we choose God's will for our life because his word is His will for our life.

The book of Isaiah 48:17 says "Thus saith the Lord, thy Redeemer, the Holy One of Israel; I am the Lord thy God which teaches thee to profit, which leadeth thee by the way that thou shouldest go."

CHAPTER 13

YOU CAN CHANGE THINGS BY WHAT YOU SAY

That's right, God's word tells you can change things by what you believe and say. When you speak and believe good – those stated in God's word—you will have good things. Conversely, if you say and believe sickness, disease, poverty, lack, and other negative things that you do not want, then these are just what you will have. The scriptures say life and death are in the power of the tongue. So study the word of God and find out what God has to say about your conditions, then say, believe and act on God's words. "And the apostles said unto the Lord, Increase our faith. And the Lord said, If ye had faith as a grain of mustard seed, ye might say unto this sycamine tree, be thou plucked up by the root, and be thou planted in the sea; and it should obey you" Luke17:5-6.

Do you get the picture now? It is important to know, believe and speak God's word. You can change things in the natural (things) you can see such as sickness, disease, poverty, and lack. Believe, speak, and have the things that God's word says you will have—health, prosperity, and success in life. That is God's word, and God's word is truth. In John 17:17, Jesus said "sanctify them through thy truth; thy word is truth."

"Death and life are in the power of the tongue… (Proverbs 18:21) and it is your tongue that must speak life if you are to have life!

Now, what do you want, the truth of God's word- health, prosperity, spiritual growth; or lies of the devil—sickness, disease, poverty, and or spiritual deficiency? You make your own heaven or hell here on earth by what you believe, speak, and do, it's up to you! "Through faith we understand that the worlds were framed by the words of God, so that things which are seen were not made of things which do appear" Hebrew 11:3. "For ever, O Lord, thy word is settled in heaven" Psalms 119:89. "The grass withereth, the flower fadeth: but the word of our God shall stand for ever" Isaiah 40:8. "While we look not at the things which are seen, but at the things which are not seen; for the things which are seen are temporal; but the things which are not seen are eternal" 11Corinthians 4:18.

CHAPTER 14

HOW TO MOVE MOUNTAINS OUT OF YOUR LIFE

"For verily I say unto you, that whosoever shall Say unto this mountain, Be thou removed, and be thou cast into the sea: and shall not doubt in his heart, but shall Believe that those things which he Saith shall come to pass; he shall have whatsoever he Saith" Mark 11:23. Speak God's word. Let His word be what comes out of your mouth, not the lies of the enemy. Remember! God's word is truth" John 17:17. Begin now, if you are not already doing so, to call those things which be not as though they were"11 Corinthians 4:18. You have what You say. So, say God's word!

Wherefore it will come to pass when the time come what you have asked for. Only the Lord establishes his word. When you receive what you ask God for be sure to pay your vow if you made one. When you ask give him thanks in advance on credit. Thank him before, during and after for what you are asking and praying for.

It is always good to lend your mouth to the Lord. Your body should be a living sacrifice to him obeying his will or word. This is when he will cause your thoughts to become agreeable to his will then so shall your plans be establish and succeed. Children should be lent to the Lord early in life.

Today our government is allowing text books in the class rooms that allow children's mind to be twisted. God's enemy is trying to take over the way we think if we are not rooted and grounded in God's word. Our hearts must rejoice in the Lord and our mouths enlarged over our enemies by rejoicing in our salvation.

The Lord is Holy and there is none beside him. There is no other foundation to build on. "Thou believest that there is one God; Thou doest well: the devils also believe, and tremble" James 2:19. We must watch how we build on the lives of our children because they are next in line to run this country. They must stand on God's solid rock because all other grounds are sinking sands. Let God's word be their knowledge because by him all our actions are weighed. God will defeat the mighty that come against him and he will make the weak strong.

Leaders are selling out by the dozens hiring themselves out for bread. In first Samuel 2:6 says "The Lord killeth, and maketh alive: he bringeth down to the grave, and bringeth up." (Vs.9), "He keep the feet of his saints, and the wicked shall be silent in darkness; for by strength shall no man prevail. (Vs.10),"The adversaries of the Lord shall be broken to pieces; out of heaven shall be thunder upon them: the Lord shall judge the ends of the earth; and he shall give strength unto his king, and exalt the horn of his anointed."

Sin is becoming great before the Lord and men and women are hating to go into the house of the Lord and there are some evil dealings like Eli's sons going on in the church. Ministers are making the people to transgress thru the traditions being taught in the church. Read 1 Samuel 2:22. In these days the word of the Lord is becoming precious because the vision of our leaders is not open. God will begin to make an end to all the choices the enemies of God are making. There seem to be no restraints and ministers don't want to preach the judgement that God bring on disobedience. There are those who are hiding the truth.

John 16:2-3 warns us that, "They shall put you out of the synagogue: yea the time cometh, that whosoever killeth you will think that he doeth God service. (Vs.3), "And these things will they do unto you, because they have not known the Father, nor me. 1 Thessalonians 4:7-8), "For God has not called us to uncleanness, but unto holiness.

(Vs.8) "He therefore that despiseth, despiseth not man, but God, who hath also given unto us his Holy Spirit." Jeremiah 6:7 talks about the wickedness of Jerusalem, "As a fountain casteth out her waters, so she casteth out her wickedness: violence and spoil is heard in her; before me continually is grief and wounds."

Our countries mind is set on vain things which cannot profit nor deliver; for they are vain. We should only fear the Lord and serve him in truth with all our heart; and remember how great he is because of all that he has done for us. If you continue to do wickedness God will consume you. All our relationships begin with how we feel about ourselves. God searches the heart. It is an inside out job.

Satan wants to keep you in the past. 1 Thessalonians 4:3, "For this is the will of God, even your sanctification that ye should abstain from fornication: We must learn how to die to sin by letting go the past or the old man and let God and his word perfect the new man. (Vs.4) "That every one of you should know how to possess his vessel in sanctification and honor."

There are too many resisting the will of God. There are consequences for being outside the will of God. Look at Jonah in his disobedience when he got caught up and afterwards was glad to do the will of God. Sin has the nature of disobedience and rebellion. If you have not been baptized and repented of your sin you are out of God's will.

There are consequences for being out of God's will. God gives you grace and that gives you time to come to him. If you die and waste your grace to hell you will go because God has given you a life time to come to him. You overlooked the most important thing you have and that is your soul. There will be no excuse because Christ is being preached all over the earth.

I pray that God help you to establish your heart to the end and that you present yourself un-blamable in holiness before God. Apostle Paul wrote while he was in jail warning the church to beware of false prophets and teachers. The Apostle Paul wrote in Philippians 1:15-18 New International Version states, (Vs.15) "It is true that some preach Christ out of envy and rivalry, but others out of goodwill. (Vs.16, "The latter do so out of love, knowing that I am put here for the defense of the gospel." (Vs.17), "The former preach Christ out of selfish ambition, not sincerely, supposing that they can stir up trouble for me while am I in chains. (Vs.18), "But what does it matter? The important thing is that in every way, whether from false motives or true, Christ is preached. And because of this I rejoice. Yes, and I will continue to rejoice."

Paul was warning us and being a watchman on the tower as an Apostle, He was warning the church to beware of false prophets and false teachers who lie. Beware of those who speak and publish in opposition to God's true prophets. Satan has followers that pretend to be Christ and shall deceive many. "For the time will come when they will not endure sound doctrine; but after their own lusts shall they heap to themselves teachers, having itching ears." "And they shall turn away their ears from the truth, and shall be turned unto fables" (2Timothy 4:3-4). They will become a product of Mental Slavery.

They will be the one who became trapped by misinformation about self and the world. We have to challenge our own way of thinking and pay attention to our own thoughts to be able to recognize when someone is polluting or corrupting our thinking with wrong teaching. John 17:17 says, "Sanctify them thru thy truth thy word is truth."

Mental Kidnapping is going forward in our government to change the minds of its citizens because Satan's agenda is to destroy, to kill and to cause to perish all of Jehovah's followers both young and old, little children and women. The wages of sin is still death. The sinner's job is or his work is to sin.

The wicked counsel that comes from Satan shall cast him down and the light of the wicked shall be put out. The gin shall take him and snares and traps are set that he has set for others he shall fall in them himself in the Mighty Name of Jesus Christ. Job 18:11 tells us that, Terrors shall make him afraid on every side and drive him to his feet."(Vs.14) of Job 18 says, "His confidence shall be rooted out of his tabernacle, and it shall bring him to the king of terrors." Read all of Job 18 and see the wages of the wicked that knoweth not God.

Bullies act as though they are a terror while they live until they die and meet "The King of Terror." Ecclesiastes 8:8 says, "There is no man that hath power over the spirit to retain the spirit; neither hath he power in the day of death: and there is no discharge in that war; neither shall wickedness deliver those that are given to it." The sinner think that he has gotten away because Ecclesiastes 8:11, reveals "Because sentence against an evil work is not executed speedily, therefore the heart of the sons of men is fully set in them to do evil." Do not cast away your confidence. (Vs.12), "Though a sinner do evil an hundred times, and his days be prolonged, yet surely I know that it shall be well with them that fear God, which fear before him."

The poet says "Woest me if my soul be wrong "Five minutes after I die." You are going to die and when you die you are either going to die in the Lord or out of the Lord. Revelation 14:13 tells us, "And I Heard a voice from heaven saying unto me, "Write, Blessed are the dead that die in the Lord from henceforth: Yea saith the Spirit, that may rest from their labors; and their works do follow them." Lamentation 3:22-23, "It is of the Lord's mercies that we are not consumed, because his compassion fails not." (Vs.23), "They are new every morning: great is thy faithfulness." Your hope in the Lord is the remedy for your soul when you hope and wait for the Lord's salvation.

God do not speak evil and good. Don't have fresh water and salt water coming up out the same fountain. "But though he cause grief, yet will he have compassion according to the multitude of his mercies" (Lamentation 3:2). When you sin your crown fall from your head "Repent" of your sin. "Preach the word; be instant in season, out of season; reprove, and rebuke, exhort with all longsuffering and doctrine." Examine yourself to see are you really in Christ or are you people pleasing. Are you following Christ and the word of God or some man made tradition? Those who are dead to sin must help pull those dead in sin out of their sin.

Ezekiel 16:17 speaks about idol worship with Dildo's. This act of lewd men and women that God will cease that of all men and women may be taught not to do after lewdness. They shall bear the sins of their idols. (Vs.17), "Thou hast also taken thy fair jewels of my gold and of my silver, which I had given thee, and madest to thyself images of men, and didst commit whoredom with them." This is God's word concerning

Dildo's. Who woman was made from, she was made for. Woman was made from man for man.

God said in Ezekiel18:4, "Behold, all souls are mine; as the soul of the father, so also the soul of the son is mine: the soul that sinneth, it shall die." When you are fornicating in your mind and heart with so called toys I have a nugget of wisdom for you in the book of Romans 6:16 that says, "Know ye not, that to whom ye yield yourselves servants to obey, his servant ye are to whom ye obey; whether of sin unto death…..or obedience unto righteousness." God created us with a mind and heart to give him glory, honor and praise with.

Read God's word so it can burn the scum out of you. There is not a person on earth that I want to go to hell with and there is nothing that I want to go to hell for. What! I'm not going to hell or jail with you. We should follow Jesus steps and that makes living holy a rough assignment. We have to endure hardness as a good soldier in Christ. Remember that even the thought of foolishness is sin.

We have to fight the good fight of faith. Lay hold of eternal life and don't let go. You can commit adultery in your mind and in a dream. Mathew 5:27-28says "Ye have heard that it was said by them of old time, Thou shalt not commit adultery; Jesus Christ brought you up to date and said in, Vs.28, "But I say unto you, That whosoever looketh on a woman to lust after her hath committed adultery with her already in his heart." This also goes for women and the use of their toys.

There is lust not just with the body, but with the heart. Jude 1:8 say filthy dreamers defile the flesh. Jeremiah 3:8, backsliding Israel committed spiritual adultery with stones and stock by bowing to them turning their backs on the living God. Things you possess and bow too that replace God with make it spiritual adultery. Setting up imagery by seeds out of Satan's mouth in heaven when he said in his heart (I will). Me, myself and I are his favorite words. There were angels in heaven that believed the seed that came out of Satan's mouth and war broke out in heaven. Words are seeds that God heard Satan speak spiritual fornication (words seeds) of rebellion. Satan sounded like your kids when they raise their voice at you to God.

This is a tough walk and I want you to remember that,
Today is a new day and it is up to you where it goes from here.
We all have one life on earth to live.
We have one life, one dance and one life chance.
God gives us grace daily to come to Him.
He gives us another opportunity to get it right.
Who's on the Lord's side?
So choose life and the blessing (Jesus Christ)
   rather than death and the curse (the devil).
Now Choose!

When there is no more community trust and cooperation divides a race or group of people that is trying to run a race from point A to point B. It is hard when it seems that the people have been put asleep. The government is controlling them legally. Mental Kidnapping is slave holding. 1 Thessalonians 4:3-6. "For this is the will of God, even your sanctification, that ye should abstain from fornication: (Vs.4), "That every one of you should know how to possess his vessel in sanctification and honour; (Vs.5), "Not in the lust of concupiscence, even as the Gentiles which know not God: (Vs.6), "That no man go beyond and defraud his brother in any matter: because that the Lord is the avenger of all such, as we also have forewarned you and testified."

Thru concupiscence brings about a wide range of sins of sexual desires. When people are isolated because of no contact with others because of Covid 19 they will think no one sees. They will have the help of Satan's merchandise like Dildos, music, T V and computers. Our world is battling with lust and concupiscence with no one to hold them accountable. The battle consist of sexual desires,, lust, lustfulness, sexual appetite, sexual longing, sexual passion, ardor, desire, passion, libido, sex drive, sexuality, biological urge, lechery, lecherousness, lasciviousness, lewdness, wantonness, carnality, licentiousness salaciousness, prurience which is paying too much attention to sex.

1 Thessalonians 5:2 says "For yourselves know perfectly that the day of the Lord so cometh as a thief in the night. This time it will be when you think you have peace and safety. We are children of the

day and we don't want to get caught with our draws down fornicating and committing adultery. "Inappropriate behavior and people want to be every-thing that they are not. Our government makes you see life upside down. We must move to be the majority to warn those who are unruly and be patient toward all men. Some ministers are chosen and controlled by the government and not by God. For instance; some black ministers are bought and sold used as a control device on the black race.

Brainwashing on those who have master degrees is still happening today. See that men don't render evil for evil. Stop compromising and telling your plans to the enemy. Defeat symbolism. Quench means to destroy, to put to an end, to cool off. There is a lot of bribes and snitching by giving an incentive by finance to tell on another. 2 Thessalonians 1:4, "So that we ourselves may glory in the churches of God for your patience and faith in all your persecution and tribulations that ye endure." Black men and women are getting shot down daily by police and blacks.

2 Thessalonians 1:7-10 states, "And to you who are troubled rest with us, when the Lord Jesus shall be revealed from heaven with his mighty angels, (Vs.8), "In flaming fire taking vengeance on them that know not God, and that obey not the gospel of our Lord Jesus Christ: (Vs.9), "Who shall punish with everlasting destruction from the presence of the Lord, and from the glory of his power; (Vs.10), "When he shall come to be glorified in his saints, and to be admired in all them that believe (because our testimony among you was believed) in that day."

Stay away from all appearance of sin. Criminals are giving the impression that they don't care about the law or prison. Sambos of America are selling out. Entertainment and those who have success have already died to us and gone to their own heaven and they don't put back or help. Sambo's of today make money off black folks. Blacks have made every ethnic group or race rich. They are not tired yet. "For we hear that there are some which walk among you disorderly, working not at all, but are busybodies."

The only race they have not made rich is themselves but they are rich in Jehovah. Today past truth is becoming a present lie. The Holy Scriptures say "Not to judge a man from the outward appearance. 1Samuel 16:7 For God does not see what man sees, for a man looks on the outward appearance, but Yaweh looks on the heart. "Look not on his countenance." Every thing that God has the devil has a counterfeit.

Women have a new therapy that looks at the outward appearance to reveal what is going on in the inside. They look like abstract painting on their face. How can the mystery of godliness in 1 Timothy 3:16 be manifest in the flesh and God's Spirit be justified through these acts? Satan uses his agents the LGBT or the alphabet group to encourage women that are blind to destroy their beauty while the male gays can take their place as the original woman. The devil is a lie.

1 Timothy 2:9-10,,14 "In like manner also, that women adorn themselves in modern apparel, with shamefacedness and sobriety; not with braided hair, or gold, or pearls, or costly array." Women are littering all over America with false hair. The government should pass laws that women when they get excited and lose their hair should put it in their purse and take it home with them. Hair and nails are part of the Jezebel movement along with abortion, lesbianism, and the increase in dildo sales.

This open rebellion against Jehovah continues from the Garden of Eden all the way up to Noah. (Vs.14) in 1 Timothy says, "And Adam was not deceived, but the woman being deceived was in the transgression." Abominable men telling women how to be women, by applying a clown face to show how they feel inside. How can the pot call the kettle black? The spirit of Satan tells homosexuals how they feel on the inside and they show it on the outward appearance. They show they are confused.

How can Satan cast out Satan? 2 Thessalonians 2:3-4 "Let no man deceive you by any means: for that day shall not come, except there come a falling away first, and that man of sin be revealed, the son of perdition; (Vs.4), "Who opposeth and exalteth himself above all that is called God, or that is worshiped; so that he as God sitteth in the temple of God, shewing himself that he is God." Our families are being broken into small pieces. Division does not make a majority but a minority. Multi-cultural is burying the black race where we will not be able to find our race in the future.

You got LBGT male and female who do gender strife oppose themselves. Pray that they recover themselves from Satan's trap those who was taken captive by his will. They became lovers of their own selves. Inappropriate behavior is not having a national plan because it is destroyed thru individuality. Our government keeps smothering the issues of the poverty of blacks. Poverty being put on people entering this country makes slaves in the work force. They are confusing and defusing. Blacks have been made a permanent minority.

Our constitution is mentally kidnapping its citizens while knocking our brains out they hold us down to go into our brains during their brain research. "But evil men and seducers shall wax worse and worse, deceiving, and being deceived"11Timothy 3:13. 11 Timothy 4:3-4 "For the time will come when they will not endure sound doctrine; but after their own lusts shall they heap to themselves teachers, having itching ears; (Vs.4) "And they shall turn away their ears from the truth, and shall be turned unto fables." They love this present world and the Lord will reward them according to their works. Their mind and conscience is defiled.

You just keep, "Looking for that blessed hope, and glorious appearing of the great God and our Savior Jesus Christ." Hebrews 1:2-4 says God, "Hath in these last days spoken unto us by his Son, whom he hath appointed heir of all things, by whom also he made the worlds; (Vs.3), "Who being the brightness of his glory, and the expressed image of his person, and upholding all things by the word of his power, when he had by himself purged our sins, sat down on the right hand of the Majesty on high. (Vs.4). "Being made so much better than the angels, as he hath by inheritance obtained a more excellent name than they." Jesus Christ is the author of eternal salvation to all who will obey him will receive the promise of eternal inheritance.

CHAPTER 15

HOLINESS WAS HERE BEFORE THE WORLD BEGAN

God is a holy God. Holiness was here before anything. 1Peter 1:15 says, "But as he which hath called you is holy, so be ye holy in all manner of conversation." Because it is written "be ye holy, for I am holy." Leviticus 11:44 "For I am the Lord your God: ye shall therefore sanctify yourselves and ye shall be holy; for I am holy: neither shall ye defile yourselves. Leviticus 20:26 says, "And ye shall be holy unto me for I the Lord am holy and have severed you from other people, that ye should be mine." In Leviticus 21:5 it talks about the Nazarites not defiling their head by not making baldness upon their head. "They shall not make baldness upon their head, neither shall they shave off the corner of their beard, nor make any cutting in their flesh."

Paul spoke differently in the New Testament where in 1 Corinthians chapter 11, about those who follow him even as he followed Christ. He was passing on what he received from Christ Jesus. He laid the order where the head of every man was Christ, the head of the woman is, not was, but is the man, and the head of Christ is God. Then he spoke about the head being covered when praying. He said that a man covering his head dishonors his head. In 1 Corinthians11:14, states, Doth not even nature itself teach you, that, if a man have long hair, it is a shame unto him." A woman not covering her head dishonors her head. A man's head not covered is a sign of subjection to God but a woman should be covered.

He revealed how the woman was created for the man and she should have power on her head because of the angels. All things are of God and we need to judge ourselves by looking at nature especially the lion and the lioness how nature itself teaches us and gave us an example from the lion and lioness. There are contentions and divisions in the church pertaining long hair and covering of the woman's hair when in 1 Corinthians 11 Paul sent by God clearly states that he has received of the Lord which also he has delivered unto us.

Now who is delivering to you? Leviticus 21:8, "Thou shalt sanctify him therefore; for he offereth the bread of thy God: he shall be holy unto thee: for I the Lord, which sanctify you, am holy" Exodus 19: 5-6 Paraphrase, expressed himself how if we would obey him we would be a peculiar treasure of people on the earth, and a kingdom of priest and a holy nation is what should be ministered to the people. 1 Thessalonians 4:7 is where God tells you he is holy and have a desire for you to be the same. "For God has not called us unto uncleanness, but unto holiness."

John (Vs.1) says, In the beginning was the Word, and the Word was with God, and the Word was God. (Vs.2) "The same was in the beginning with God." And He is a holy God. So holiness was here before the world began. The Wisdom of God and His word have creative power. Hebrews 1:10-12 tells us "And, Thou, Lord, in the beginning hast laid the foundation of the earth; and the heavens are the works of thine hands: (Vs.11), They shall perish; but thou remainest; and they all shall wax old as doth a garment; (Vs.12), "And as a vesture shalt thou fold them up, and they shall be changed: but thou art the same, and thy years shall not change."

God's word is the same today, yesterday and forever more and it never changes not even for the Supreme Courts. God's love for us was before the world began. What was written for saints is being turned around or reversed by men who die. These men are nothing but dust and worms. God's grace and mercy is too good for those who have a backward behavior.

2Thessalonians 2:10-14,16 KJV, reminds us that, "And with all deceivableness of unrighteousness in them that perish; because they received not the love of the truth, that they might not be saved. (Vs.11), "And for this cause God shall send them strong delusion, that they should believe a lie: (Vs.12), "That they all might be damned who believed not the truth, but had pleasure in unrighteousness. (Vs.13), "But we are bound to give thanks always to God for you, brethren beloved of the Lord, because God hath from the beginning chosen you to salvation through sanctification of the Spirit and belief of the truth: (Vs.14), "Whereunto he called you by our gospel, to the obtaining of the glory of our Lord Jesus Christ." (Vs.16) "Now our Lord Jesus Christ himself, and God, even our Father, which hath loved us, and hath given us everlasting consolation, and good hope through grace."

CHAPTER 16

SCRIPTURES: OF THE MYSTERY OF JESUS CHRIST AS GOD AND FATHER

2 Timothy 1:9 tells us, "Who hath saved us, and called us with an holy calling, not according to our works, but according to his own purpose and grace, which was given us in Christ Jesus before the world began." Titus 1:2, "In hope of eternal, which God, that cannot lie, promised before the world began." Luke 1:70, "As he spake by the mouth of his prophets, which have been since the world began." Romans 16:25, "Now to him that is of power to stablish you according to my gospel, and the preaching of Jesus Christ, according to the revelation of the mystery, which was kept secret since the world began."

Corinthians 12:7, "But we speak the wisdom of God in a mystery, {even} the hidden {Wisdom}, which God ordained before the world unto his glory." Ephesian 3:4, "Whereby, when ye read, ye may understand my knowledge in the mystery of Christ. Ephesian 1:9, "Having made known unto us the mystery of his will, according to his good pleasure which he hath purposed in himself. Ephesians 3:3, "How that by revelation he made known unto me the mystery; (as I wrote afore in few words, Ephesians 3:4 "Whereby; when ye read, ye may understand my knowledge in the mystery of Christ)

Ephesians 3:5, "Which in other ages was not known unto the sons of men, as it is now revealed unto his holy apostles and prophets by the Spirit. Ephesians 3:9, "And to make all men see what is the fellowship of the mystery, which from the beginning of the world hath been hid in God, who created all things by Jesus Christ. Jesus Christ in 1Peter 1:20, "Who verily was foreordained before the foundation of the world, but was manifest in these last times for you." Jesus Christ the Bishop of our soul in 1 Peter 2:25 that we may live in him. "Ye also, as living stones, are built up a spiritual house, an holy priesthood, to offer up spiritual sacrifices, acceptable to God by Jesus Christ." We do this because God is Spirit and those who worship him must worship him in spirit and in truth.

CHAPTER 17

COWARDS

There are those who have already turned aside to Satan believing the science. 1 Timothy 4:1 tells us that, "Now the Spirit speaketh expressly that in the latter times some shall depart from the faith, giving heed to seducing spirits and doctrine of devils" 1Timothy 4:1. 2 Peter 2:2-3, "And many shall follow their pernicious ways; by reason of whom the way of truth shall be evil spoken of. (Vs.3), "And through covetousness shall they feigned words make merchandise of you: whose judgement now of a long time lingereth not, and their damnation slumbereth not." (Vs 9), "The Lord knoweth how to deliver the Godly out of temptations, and to reserve the unjust unto the day of judgement to be punished."

Continue: (Vs.10), in 2 Peter 2 says, "But chiefly them that walk after the flesh in lust of uncleanness, and despise government. Presumptuous are they, self-willed, they are not afraid to speak evil of dignities." They practice covetousness and cursed their children who have forsaken the right way and who love the wages of unrighteousness which is death. "The wages of sin is death. " God does not want anybody to perish but that all should come to repentance.

Jehovah has fire reserved for the heavens and the earth and holiness in those being like Christ will be the survivors. Just think the heavens will be on fire and will be dissolved. 11Peter 3:12-13, "Looking for and hasting unto the coming of the day of God, wherein the heavens being on fire shall be dissolved, and the elements shall melt with fervent heat." (Vs13, "Nevertheless we, according to his promise, look for new heaven and a new earth, wherein dwellest righteousness."

Those who are unlearned and unstable that rest and do not understand the scriptures it shall be unto their own destruction. They run, duck and hide from the presence of the Lord and his goodness. They are wondering why they are still alive to only realize they have wasted God's grace. He was only giving you what you did not deserve and that was another day to get it right and come to him. We must all be careful not to be led away into the ways of the wicked. When we think we stand, we must take heed unless we fall.

We have passed from darkness to light. When we got saved the darkness has passed away and the true light will shine in us because we know Jesus Christ who is the True Light from the beginning. We should love not the world neither the things that are in the world like the lust of the flesh, the lust of the eye, and the pride of life. All lust will pass away but those who do the will of him who is from the beginning will abide forever. There are many deceivers or anti-christ in our world who is among us and many that have walked away from the church. "They went out from us, but they were not all of us; for if they had been of us, they would no doubt have continued with us: but they went out, that they might be made manifest that were not all of us" 1John 2:19.

They know not the truth about Jesus Christ and have denied that Jesus is the Christ. We have all sinned and we must have the Father and the Son. 'If we say we have no sin we deceive ourselves, and the truth is not in us." A lot of people want to acknowledge the Father but not the Son. Be steadfast in the Father and the Son because this is our promise to eternal life. We must abide in the anointing that we have received from Christ who means anointing.

Jesus Christ knows his sheep and his sheep hear his voice. Jesus Christ was manifested to take away our sin because he had no sin. "Beloved, now are we the sons of God, and it doth not yet appear what we should be: but we know that, when he shall appear, we shall be like him; for we shall see him as he is" 1 John 3:2. There are a lot of people in the church who really don't know Jesus Christ personally. They never got their god straight. In order to worship God you must first know who he is. You have to know him for yourself. Stay in his word until he reveals himself to you. After you are baptized ask God to give you his Holy Spirit to live inside you. Hebrews 12:14 tells us to, "Follow peace with all men, and holiness, without which no man shall see the Lord."

Examine yourself and know if you be Christ's because his spiritual seed will be in you with the evidence of speaking in tongues. If you are born of God it will bother you when you commit sin. We should also love one another. Remember when you kill your brother like Cain you also kill yourself. When you kill your brother you become a murderer and know murderer has eternal life abiding in him. We should love in deed and truth. We will know we are his by the spirit that he has given us to abide in us. Every spirit that confesseth that Jesus Christ is come in the flesh is of God. This is how you know the Spirit of God is in you and others.

Those who are not of God don't want to hear about God but we must love them anyway. 1 John 4:7-8 says "Beloved, let us love one another: for love is of God: and every one that loveth is born of God, and knoweth God. (Vs8), "He that loveth not knoweth not God; for God is love. God sent his Son Jesus to manifest himself in us so that we could live through him. Reading and meditating on God's word feeds his Spirit on the inside of us developing our spirit man so we can become Christ like. 1 John 4:15, "Whosoever shall confess that Jesus is the Son of God, God is in him and he is in God."

Remember that there is no fear in love because perfect love cast out fear. We believe that Jesus Christ is born of God. Jesus came to overcome the world by faith so we can be rooted and grounded in love so we could be filled with all the fullness of God. He came by water and blood and his Spirit beareth witness because he gave us the spirit of truth. "I am Alpha and Omega, the beginning and the ending, saith the Lord, which is, and which was, and which is to come, the Almighty. God is spirit, "which is" and he was in the body that died when he gave up the ghost at the cross. This is when he was "which was" because the flesh died but God the spirit cannot die.

He is also spirit when he will return on a cloud "which is to come." On earth there are three that bear witness on earth, the Spirit, and the water and the blood and these three agree in one. The life of the flesh is the blood and at the cross blood and water came out. The body was dead and placed in the tomb but the spirit left that body and went to preach to the spirits in prison. The body or flesh can only be in one place at a time but the spirit can be everywhere. God's spirit was in Jesus on earth and God who is spirit was in heaven. 1 John 5:13 says, "These things have I written unto you that believe on the name of the son of God; that ye may know that ye have eternal life, and that ye may believe on the name of the Son of God.

1 John 5:20 reminds us "And we know that the Son of God is come, and hath given us an understanding, that we may know him that is true, and we are in him that is true, even in his Son Jesus Christ. This is the true God, and eternal life." Let this be your confidence and let it be for the truth sake that dwelleth in us. "Thou art worthy, O Lord, to receive glory and honour and power: for thou hast created all things, and for thy pleasure they are and were created" Revelation 4:11.

Our victory over Satan is in Christ Jesus. We overcame him (the devil) (1) By the blood of the Lamb and (2) by the words of our testimony. By our spreading of the everlasting gospel with courage and patience in suffering and not loving our lives unto death. The love for our own life was overcome by a stronger affections of another nature from the boldness of the (Holy Ghost) that was the character of Jehovah given to us. Our love perfected helped us defeat the monster of our imagination or the beast.

Our obedience to Jehovah helps us to resist the devil and the multitude of his merchandise. Since he don't have power over us nor in heaven all he can do is blasphemy and distract us to make some fall in his short limited time. He has power over those whose name is not written in the Lambs Book of Life. The pretense of religion shall deceive the souls of many by drawing away humankind from worshipping the one true God. I am a miracle and I believe that miracles still happen today. Pretending and playing church as they are deceiving their own-selves. He is using lying wonders, pretended miracles as you see people get up out of wheel chairs faking healing. He used ministers to pretend. Satan is working in men and women that use pretense. They are pretending.

There are some who worship in Satan's temple that make open profession of their subjection to him. These Satanic Temples are presenting themselves to the Capital and want to build statues on the Capital grounds to show religious freedom. In the Bible Belt section of the country there are Temples called Friends of the Satanic Temple in Memphis Tennessee. Atheist are those who have an absence of belief in God are coming out of the closet to show the world that they are proud to be hell bound. Psalms 14:1, "The fool has said in his heart, "There is no God." Wiccan another godless group is expanding territory. Satanic group set out to kill more babies in Texas with abortion. Kids are starting after school Satanic groups.

The winged goat statue of Baphomet want it first amendment right in Arkansas. They are attempting to set Baal next to the Ark in the capital in Arkansas. Satan has his agents out in full force. The Truth will be standing tall after all the lies have been told. Just stand firm in God's Spirit centering in on the Gospels work because Satan's days are numbered and the Lamb shall overcome. The King of kings and the Lord of lords who rules in heaven, on earth and in hell is still in full control.

God's followers are called, chosen and faithful. God has aggrandized or increased the power, status, and wealth of them. The wealth of the wicked is laid up for the just. The power of God that influenced the minds of our leaders as he did Pharaoh in Egypt hardens their hearts to sin. We wonder how could our government pass such laws but it was the powerful influence that God have on their minds. God uses whomever he chooses to do his will and so do Satan when you allow him to use you. Babylon has fallen, has fallen. The atmosphere of our world is full of unclean spirits and people are rejecting the one true God by the worship of idols called spiritual adultery. These spirits draw them away from God using lust, money, wealth and luxury to hold their interest.

If you want God's mercy you must come out of her, the world affiliates. If not you will be strengthening and assisting the hand of evil doers. Those who hold on to their pride will be caught off guard when

Jesus comes like a thief in the night. You can now see the reward of the wicked. Those who look at their fall from a distance will be similar to the rich man and Lazarus where the guffix separated them in Luke sixteen. Thank God that he keeps us separate and set apart. Those who sold you products to help you fall into sin and got rich off you will look at you from afar off as they are punished. The spirit of the antichrist is a worldly spirit and will have a worldly sorrow.

The world will only fall into calamity but God's church will rise again. There will be a marriage song with angels and the righteousness of saints and a feast made up of the promises of the gospel the true saying of God. When the apostles fell down at the angels feet and the angel said that I am a fellow servant and of thy brethren which have the testimony of Jesus. We Worship God and him alone. We worship Jesus Christ the Word of God made flesh. We use the sharp sword of his mouth to do battle. His word is the weapon of our warfare.

The devil, the false prophet and the beast will be cast into the lake of fire to be tormented day and night forever and ever. The strength and subtlety of the serpent will not be enough to deliver himself from the bottomless pit. The only ones secured from the second death will be those who are holy. God's servants are blessed and holy. The great day of judgement is coming soon where we all will appear before the judgement- seat of Christ. No matter how rich you are or what your title is here on earth you will not be able to flee from this court. There will be nowhere to run, nor hide to flee from the wrath to come.

Jehovah gave everybody grace and that is a chance to come to him. Even those who said tomorrow and tomorrow never came because it is always a day ahead. They did not receive him as Savior, so now they will have to meet him as judge. They can't get away from Jesus Christ because they are going to meet him as Savior or as Judge, but they are going to meet him. When you did not choose God you made an automatic covenant with death and an agreement with hell. Those who chose Jesus as Lord and savior were justified and acquitted by the judge.

Romans 2:4-5 tells us that God's patience has a limit. If you are testing the patience of God you need to stop and think and stop trying to explain the truth away. Romans 2:4-5 says, "Or despisest thou the riches of his goodness and forbearance and longsuffering; not knowing that the goodness of God leadeth thee to repentance? (Vs.5), "But after thy hardness and impenitent heart treasurest up unto thyself wrath against the day of wrath and revelation of the righteous judgement of God; (Vs. 6), "Who will render to every man according to his deeds."

ABOUT THE AUTHOR

Steven Treadwell is a noted author and a man chosen by God to encourage, uplift and motivate those I came in contact with the unadulterated, uncompromising, unchanging word of God. He was born in Memphis Tenn. Where he graduated from George Washington Carver High. He started to serve God at an early age being baptized at the age of 10.He sung in the choir at church and Jr high school, high school and on to college. He studied Sociology and song the college choir under Omar Robinson the mastro of music for a year and a half at Shelby State now called Southwest Tenn. College. He transferred from Shelby State to Philander Smith in Little Rock Arkansas studying Sociology and singing with choir.Steven Treadwell's mission has always been the motivator the one that provides a reason to do something., always motivating the people. He is the encourager of the brethren sharing courage and confidence. This is when he moved to Los Angeles Ca. and I begin to study the teaching of Fredrick K Price at Crenshaw Christian Center where my revelation to the word of God began. I began to walk by faith and not by sight. I was not afraid of what I saw or heard. I became conscience about what I said. I studied real estate briefly at West Los Angeles in Culver City Ca. I was in the city of angels with a devil's heart and don't take that likely. While working across from CBS on Beverly Blvd and Fairfax, I rubbed shoulders with the stars that gave me a larger than life picture of myself. This florist driver had a great job that kept me on the scene in L A Ca. I left California and moved to Atlanta attending a small business college called Rutledge. I used my outreach to try and save a struggling school, but it was too late. I returned to Memphis after sharing my teaching that I acquired from Crenshaw Christian Center to Atlanta now to Memphis. I studied more and evangelized at Northwest College South haven Mississippi. University of Phoenix, Strayer University and the University of Memphis. I am now writing my second book still providing a reason to do something with courage and confidence.

www.ingramcontent.com/pod-product-compliance
Lightning Source LLC
LaVergne TN
LVHW092053060526
838201LV00047B/1377